MARK TWAIN IN GERMANY

Number Nine of the

COLUMBIA UNIVERSITY GERMANIC STUDIES

Edited by Robert Herndon Fife

New Series

MARK TWAIN
IN GERMANY

EDGAR H. HEMMINGHAUS

AMS PRESS, INC.
NEW YORK
1966

To Nola

PREFACE

The author takes this opportunity to acknowledge his great indebtedness to all those who aided him in the preparation of this study.

He is deeply grateful to the Preussische Staatsbibliothek, the Auskunftsbureau der Deutschen Bibliotheken, and the Amerika-Institut in Berlin, the Deutsche Bücherei in Leipsic, and the Columbia University Library in New York City for the many courtesies accorded him. The Preussische Staatsbibliothek in Berlin and the Deutsche Bücherei in Leipsic kindly furnished him with photostatic material.

He wishes also to thank Dr. Wilhelm Frels of the Deutsche Bücherei in Leipsic for bibliographical assistance; Mr. Ulrich Steindorff for his generous help and interest; Herr Otto Schramm, Lutz Verlag of Stuttgart, and many publishing firms in Germany, Austria, and Switzerland for pertinent information in regard to the sale and distribution of Mark Twain's works in Germany; Professor P. Grossmann of the Amerika-Institut in Berlin, Mr. Albert Deane, Director of Foreign Advertisement and Publicity, Paramount Pictures Inc., and the Department of Commerce in Washington, D.C. for data on the Mark Twain films in Germany; and Dr. Günther Keil for valuable suggestions and for his aid in reading the proof. Furthermore, he wishes to express his appreciation to Professor Frederick W. J. Heuser, who read the manuscript with minute care and offered much valuable advice.

Above all, however, he owes a special debt of gratitude to Professor Robert Herndon Fife who suggested to him the possibilities of the present subject. Professor Fife's scholarly guidance and constant encouragement through every phase of this investigation have alone made possible the completion of this study.

E. H. H.

CONTENTS

INTRODUCTION

An expanding knowledge of America and growing interest in its character and fortunes[1] began to show themselves in Germany at the time of the American Revolution and developed in the literature toward the end of the century into a romantic enthusiasm for the primitive nature of this continent and its aboriginal inhabitants. A great stimulus of interest in the American people and their culture came after the Wars of Liberation, when economic hardships and political unrest drove thousands of German subjects to flee from the homeland and take refuge in this country. The promotion of this closer relationship between America and Germany then gradually developed a more realistic knowledge of the American people among German authors and a keener interest in the American picture on the part of the German reading public. This was accompanied by an increase in German books and articles in periodicals dealing with life and character on this side of the ocean. As the War of Secession approached, writers from Berthold Auerbach to Ernst Adolf Willkomm brought America into the background of their stories. Some of these authors, like Sealsfield and Gerstäcker, knew the American scene at first hand. Others drew their knowledge from the many descriptions by German travelers of this era or the more or less biased accounts of returning emigrants, while still others derived their picture from the older romantic tradition or drew from pure imagination.

In the meantime the way had been opened to translations of American authors. Cooper, Irving, Poe, Hawthorne, Longfellow, and others of the older school of American literature found their way to the German public as a whole or in individual works. As yet literary critics had little to say, but the warm reception accorded American novels[2] and sketches as evidenced by repeated

[1] Cf. for the period, Paul C. Weber, *America in Imaginative German Literature in the First Half of the Nineteenth Century* (Columbia University Press, 1926) for sources.

[2] For a detailed discussion of the reception of the American novel in Germany in these early years, see Lawrence Marsdon Price, *The Reception of English Literature in Germany* (Berkeley: University of California Press, 1932), pp. 423-435. Also Clement Vollmer, *The American Novel in Germany, 1871-1913* (Philadelphia: International Printing Co., 1918), pp. 11 f.

reprintings showed that the German reading public was taking a genuine interest. It can hardly have been a curious interest in the exotic alone that caused so wide a distribution of the older American novels. There must have been a real appreciation on the part of German readers that these story tellers from the New World had the imagination and the stylistic power to make a distinctive contribution to the literature of the world.

The German reader was therefore fully prepared to greet the new American school of fiction that rose after 1870. Here Bret Harte opened the way, with his colorful and humorous stories of the Western frontier. Then in 1875 Mark Twain's *The Innocents Abroad* appeared in German dress. Thus introduced, America's great humorist entered on a career in Germany which has lasted to the present time. Rising slowly on the horizon, then developing rapidly to personal and literary popularity, Mark Twain has had his high points and his depressions, but during the more than two generations since his first work came from the German press the American writer has at no time ceased to occupy the attention of readers and critics.

The reception of Mark Twain in Germany has by no means been utterly disregarded. Several friendly critics have touched upon this subject. Archibald Henderson, an American critic, in his study *Mark Twain*[3] analyzes Mark Twain's reception in various European countries; but merely a few pages[4] are devoted to his reception among the "Germanic peoples." He calls attention to "the lavish entertainment and open-hearted homage" bestowed upon him by German Europe, and quoting with approval from various critics as representative of German opinion, confines himself to a very brief exposition of those elements in Mark Twain that appealed or did not appeal to the "Germanic consciousness." The German critic, Friedrich Schönemann, in the opening chapter[5] of his monograph *Mark Twain als literarische Persönlichkeit,*[6]

[3] New York: Frederick A. Stokes Company, 1910.
[4] Henderson, *op. cit.*, pp. 139-145. See also *The North American Review*, CXCII (Dec., 1910), 805-815, for his article, "The International Fame of Mark Twain." Aside from a few additions, this article is almost identical in content with that mentioned above.
[5] This chapter carried the title "Mark Twain in der Kritik."
[6] *Jenaer Germanistische Forschungen*, Jena: Verlag der Frommannschen Buchhandlung, 1925.

limits himself to a few pertinent observations. German reception
of Mark Twain, in his opinion, had the advantage of freedom from
the racial and mental restraints of the French and the political
and cultural susceptibilities of the English. In their admiration for
"das Fremde," German critics were, to be sure, inclined to over-
statement. Furthermore, they interpreted Mark Twain's humor
as a form of expression and disregarded the content of his works
as well as his whole personality as the human and spiritual basis
of his activity.

Valuable as these observations may be, they do little more than
touch on the problem. No systematic effort has previously been
made to explore with any degree of thoroughness the German
view of Mark Twain in its historical features. The purpose of
the present study is to trace, as far as the available source material
permits, the development of German interest in the works of Mark
Twain from 1874 to the present. It does not include an examination of the influence of Mark Twain on German literature. It seeks
to present a somewhat clearly defined picture of the reception of
Mark Twain by the German public and German critics. This
implies an examination of two classes of sources: first, the publication of translations of Mark Twain's works in Germany as a
quantitative index of his popularity among German readers, and
second, the critical introductions of the various editions, reviews,
literary essays and histories, monographs including newspaper
articles, in which the author and his works were interpreted and
criticized. These two approaches to the question will be found to
supplement each other. It has been remarked more than once by
German writers that the critical material on Mark Twain is somewhat disappointing in quality and this will be found substantiated
in the following pages. At various crises during the period under
investigation it will be noted that the data respecting the issue of
his works and their extensive sale seems to be a more responsive
index to his popularity than the opinion of the critics.

In view of the fact that the reception of an author, be he native
or foreign, is never stationary but tends to show a rise or a decline
in interest, the most satisfactory method of approach for a study
of this character is manifestly chronological. A difficulty arises in
determining the lines of demarcation. From a study of the material

it became evident that divisions were possible neither solely on
the basis of outer criteria, such as the biographical crises, nor
solely on the basis of inner criteria, such as shifts of German
critical opinion. Both had to be taken into consideration. In
general it was found most convenient to divide the German reception of Mark Twain into two parts: that of the pre-war and that
of the post-war period. As it happened, the pre-war reception,
taken as a whole, ended with the death of Mark Twain. This was
of primary importance inasmuch as Mark Twain was an author
whose personality played a dominant rôle in the German attitude
towards his work. Chapter I seeks to trace the steps by which he
gained a foothold in Germany. The years embraced in this analysis
extend from 1874 to 1891. With Mark Twain's second visit to
Germany in the latter year, German enthusiasm for him gains
momentum. Chapter II, then, examines the factors that enabled
him to consolidate and strengthen his prestige in the years that
followed. Chapter III seeks to evaluate the press appraisals, which
were generally favorable, and the eulogies that followed his seventieth anniversary in 1905 and his death in 1910, as well as the
German attitude in the intervening years. Chapter IV concludes
the analysis of the pre-war reception, and includes a discussion
of German interest in American appraisements of Mark Twain.
The post-war reception shows a decided renascence in public
interest. Although Mark Twain's reputation suffered a temporary
eclipse, comparatively speaking, in the years of the World War,
it emerged considerably stronger in the period immediately following. Chapter V takes note of this revival of interest and of the
conflicting views of the author by German critics between 1919
and 1925. Chapter VI deals primarily with the critical appreciation
of Mark Twain's literary personality by the outstanding German
specialist in Mark Twain, Friedrich Schönemann, and with the
resulting dissenting opinions. Chapter VII examines the gradual
diminution of interest that followed the post-bellum vogue and
became more and more observable as the years went by; while
Chapter VIII, in conclusion, analyzes the numerous centennial
appreciations of 1935.

The term *German* has been used in this study with considerable latitude. It implies not merely Great Germany, as it is now constituted, but also the areas of German speech in Switzerland and Hungary, in short, *German Europe*.

As regards the periodical press, the selection of material for investigation offered a problem, as it does in all researches of this character. A diligent examination of the journals, including newspapers accustomed to publish literary *feuilletons* of importance, disclosed that the following were the chief sources which yielded material of interest: *Anglia: Beiblatt, Allgemeine Zeitung, Beilage* (Munich), *Alte und neue Welt, Archiv für das Studium der neueren Sprachen, Deutsche Rundschau, Das literarische Echo, Deutsche Literaturzeitung, Die Gegenwart, Die Literatur, Die Neueren Sprachen, Die Zukunft, Englische Studien, Frankfurter Zeitung, Germanisch-Romanische Monatsschrift, Hamburger Nachrichten, Hochschule und Ausland, Illustrierte Zeitung, Leipziger Neueste Nachrichten, Magazin für die Literatur des Auslandes, März, National-Zeitung* (Berlin), *Neue Freie Presse, Neues Wiener Tagblatt, Tägliche Rundschau, Velhagen & Klasings Monatshefte, Vossische Zeitung, Wiener Deutsches Tagblatt,* and *Zeitschrift für französischen und englischen Unterricht.*

Some of the periodicals were obtained at the Columbia University Library and by loan from other American and European libraries. However, the greater part had to be sought in the Berlin Staatsbibliothek and the Deutsche Bücherei at Leipsic.

PART ONE

PRE-WAR RECEPTION

I

EARLY RECEPTION
1874-1891

"Amerikanische Humoristen" (Grunow)——Tauchnitz——"Sternbanner-Serie" (Lutz)——Schönbach——Engel——Literary historians: Scherr, Doehn, Engel, Körting, Bierbaum, Knortz——Analysis of Mark Twain's humor——Summary.

In 1873 the firm of Friedrich Wilhelm Grunow in Leipsic published a translation of the first of three volumes of Bret Harte's *The Tales of the Argonauts* under the title *Die Argonauten-Geschichten.* The principal objective was to measure, if at all possible, the strength of public interest in American fiction. What the actual reaction of the reading public would be, was extremely questionable, for there were obstacles that could not be ignored. The immediate problems of economy and politics in Germany created a formidable barrier. Germany was still more or less engaged in the complicated process of readjusting herself after her war with France, and in the equally intricate task of establishing the German Empire. But contrary to expectation, the German public "awakened to the charms of Bret Harte's Far West, with its gold mines and its motley adventurous throng." The manifestation of a general interest in this work convinced the publisher that it was also a most propitious moment to introduce Mark Twain. Within the brief period of four years Grunow published in rapid succession six volumes of Mark Twain's works in German translation as part of a very impressive series, "Amerikanische Humoristen."[1] The first volume,[2] which consisted of the story of the Jumping Frog, numerous satirical essays and sketches, and the book of travel, *Roughing It,* appeared in 1874 under the title *Jim Smileys berühmter Springfrosch und dergleichen wunderliche Käuze mehr. Im Silberlande Nevada.* The following year brought a translation of *The Innocents Abroad* in two volumes,[3] the first

[1] The entire series consisted of twelve volumes: two by Artemus Ward, two by Aldrich, one by Max Adeler, six by Mark Twain, and one by Mark Twain and Charles Dudley Warner.
[2] Vol. II of the series.
[3] Vols. IV and V of the series.

under the title *Die Arglosen auf Reisen* and the second as *Die neue Pilgerfahrt.* In 1876 Grunow issued two further volumes, the one a translation of *The Gilded Age,* with the German title *Das vergoldete Zeitalter,*[4] the other a translation of *The Adventures of Tom Sawyer,* entitled *Tom Sawyer. Eine Jugendgeschichte.*[5] The year 1877 marked the completion of the series with a German version of *Sketches New and Old,* called *Skizzenbuch.*[6] There is no doubt that the sketches proved a very popular book, for Reclam published a cheap edition of some ten of Mark Twain's sketches the following year under the title *Ausgewählte Skizzen.*[7]

It was a fortunate turn of circumstances that the translator who introduced Mark Twain to the Germans was the eminent publicist Moritz Busch. Busch had studied theology and philosophy at the University of Leipsic and had acquired a reputation as a translator of Dickens, Thackeray, and other English authors. A strong exponent of republicanism, he visited America in 1851 in the hope that he might find there the fulfillment of his cherished ideals of freedom. The following year, however, he returned disillusioned to Germany. He became associated with the *Grenzboten,* one of the most influential German periodicals in the field of politics, literature, and art, then under the editorship of Gustav Freytag. In 1870 he received an appointment in the German Foreign Office, but his real function was that of an intermediary with the press for Prince Bismarck. Up to the year 1874 Busch's life was one of unusual activity. But in spite of his laborious political and journalistic duties, he retained an intense interest in literature. His training and experience qualified him fully to interpret America through Mark Twain.

The service of Busch and the Grunow firm in their effort to familiarize the German public with one of the foremost American humorists was immediately acknowledged by critics in the German press. The *Neue Freie Presse* and the *Norddeutsche Allgemeine Zeitung* expressed their unqualified approval, characterizing the

[4] Vols. VI and VII of the series.
[5] Vol. XI of the series.
[6] Vol. XII of the series.
[7] These sketches were translated by a Wilhelm Lange, who in succeeding years was to distinguish himself with translations from the Romance, Germanic, and Slavic languages. He is also credited with various adaptations of Björnson's dramas.

project as a literary event of magnitude; and a Dr. Friedmann,[8] in a review[9] of the initial volume, even referred to it as *epoche-machend*. These appraisals, brief though they were, did not overlook the merit of the translation as an incentive to a concrete interest in Mark Twain. The spirit of the original, Friedmann says, is reproduced faithfully, and the naïve humor of the language —a humor which is frequently discernible only between the lines —is retained with fine understanding. A standard, a "classical" translation, he calls it, which bears favorable comparison with the excellent rendering of Dickens by Julius Seybt and others.

We may assume that the public response to these early volumes was quite favorable, for soon after their publication the rising vogue of Mark Twain was evidenced by his incorporation into the Tauchnitz Library. The Tauchnitz firm, founded in Leipsic in 1837, was noted for its accurate classical and Biblical texts, its dictionaries, and other works of reference. In 1841 Tauchnitz began a "Collection of British Authors" with the purpose of familiarizing the German public with the literary productions of English and American novelists. This collection, augmented each year, was widely read on the Continent. To find publication in the Tauchnitz series was in itself a recognition of an author's merit. Beginning with 1876, Tauchnitz issued an English edition of Mark Twain's *The Adventures of Tom Sawyer*[10] and followed it with other Mark Twain volumes as they appeared.[11]

---

[8] Dr. Friedmann was a frequent contributor of essays and reviews in the field of the drama and the novel. These appeared in the *Magazin für die Literatur des Auslandes*, cited hereafter as *MfdLdA*.

[9] *MfdLdA*, April 22, 1876, pp. 241 f.

[10] This work was issued in book form in America in December, 1876.

[11] Two volumes of *The Innocents Abroad* appeared in 1879, *Roughing It* and two volumes of *A Tramp Abroad* in 1880. Tauchnitz, in a letter to Mark Twain, proposed to issue an illustrated edition of this work in Germany, besides putting it into his regular series. Apparently nothing came of this suggestion. Cf. Albert Bigelow Paine, *Mark Twain, a Biography* (New York: Harper & Brothers Publishers, 1912), II, 666. The year 1881 brought *Innocents at Home* and two volumes of *The Prince and the Pauper;* 1882, *The Stolen White Elephant and Other Stories;* 1883, one volume of *Sketches* and two volumes of *Life on the Mississippi;* 1885, two volumes of *The Adventures of Huckleberry Finn (Tom Sawyer's Comrade);* 1886, *Selections from American Humour;* and 1890, two volumes of *A Connecticut Yankee in King Arthur's Court (A Yankee at the Court of King Arthur)*. Though the law did not require Tauchnitz to pay Mark Twain for the privilege of publication, he nevertheless paid "of his own will and accord" all that he could afford to pay (Paine, *op. cit.*, II, 643).

To what extent these editions were read by various classes is difficult to ascertain. The Tauchnitz volumes supplied those whose education had given them a reading knowledge of English, but we may safely conclude that their number was exceedingly limited. The great bulk of the German public became acquainted with Mark Twain through the translations.[12]

One of the most important publishing houses to associate itself with the movement to create and perpetuate an interest in the American humorist through translation was the Stuttgart firm of Robert Lutz. Inspired by a desire to promote a better understanding between Germany and America, Lutz undertook a noteworthy project in the publication of a series of twelve volumes devoted to American humorists and novelists, known as the "Sternbanner-Serie." Of these twelve volumes, three were devoted to Mark Twain. The first of these appeared in 1886[13] under the picturesque title *Unterwegs und Daheim*. Here the young publisher presented for the first time in a German translation a select group of Mark Twain's humorous sketches. As the title might suggest, *Unterwegs* consists of those sketches which originated on the author's travels through Germany, France, and Switzerland, while *Daheim* presents those *humoresques* which sprang from the native soil. The sketches were translated by various individuals, the most prominent among them being Udo Brachvogel and Margarete Jacobi. Brachvogel had spent many years of his life in America and had repeatedly interpreted not only American authors but also various phases of American life in his poems.[14] Margarete

---

[12] In analyzing the factors that explain Mark Twain's reception in Germany in these early years one must not forget the importance of his first visit, in 1878. Paine (*op. cit.*, II, 616-640) gives an interesting description of this sojourn in Germany and Switzerland. Wherever he went, we are told, Mark Twain was the center of attraction. The warm affection which he displayed towards the Germans was returned by them. But whether this interest in his person led to a corresponding interest in his books cannot be definitely determined; it is plausible to assume that it did in some instances. One fact, however, stands out clearly—the name of Mark Twain became known to an increasingly larger circle.

[13] Vol. II of the series.

[14] After a brief residence in Vienna and Hungary, Brachvogel emigrated in 1867 to the United States, where he lived until his death in 1913. For years he was associated with German-American newspapers either as correspondent or editor, and contributed frequently to various literary journals here and abroad. His reputation as an author rests mainly on his volume of German verse, entitled *Gedichte* (1912),

Jacobi, for her part, had gained considerable distinction as a translator from the French, Italian, and English.[15]

The second of the Mark Twain volumes, *Leben auf dem Mississippi*,[16] was translated by Udo Brachvogel and Francis Siller, and appeared two years later, in 1888. Like Brachvogel, Siller was also a feuilletonist and a translator of no mean repute.[17] Robert Lutz realized that *Life on the Mississippi* contained much material that obviously would be of little interest to the German reader. Only that portion of the book was translated which treated of the author's life as a pilot on the Mississippi; the second part, which describes the tremendous changes along the Mississippi after the Civil War, was too much concerned with local conditions. Inasmuch as *Life on the Mississippi* contains an important chapter in the life of the author, Lutz found it expedient to place before the German reader in an introductory chapter an interesting biographical sketch of the "oft-mentioned but little known author."

The third Mark Twain volume of the series brought a translation by Henny Koch[18] of *The Adventures of Huckleberry Finn* under the title *Abenteuer und Fahrten des Huckleberry Finn*.[19] An English edition had appeared in the Tauchnitz Library in 1885, yet a period of five years elapsed before it was rendered into German. This does not mean, however, that publishers ignored

a collection of the best of his many scattered ballads and metrical translations. His artistic skill as a translator is exhibited in selections from Longfellow, Poe, Whittier, Bayard Taylor, Hawthorne, and others. The most ambitious among his prose translations is said to be his rendering of Bret Harte's *Gabriel Conroy*, published in 1876 (Stuttgart), a year after the appearance of the original.

[15] Prior to 1886, Margarete Jacobi had established herself as an author of some note with two novels, *Immergrün* (1884) and *Unsre Festzeiten* (1885). Her interest in contemporary American literature led her to publish for German youth an adaptation of Stowe's *Uncle Tom's Cabin*. Recognition of her skill as a translator is shown by the fact that she was commissioned to furnish translations for four additional volumes of the "Sternbanner-Serie."

[16] Vol. V of the series.

[17] Siller was born in St.Petersburg in 1835, spent several years in Germany, and then emigrated to the United States, where he died in 1901. He interpreted American life in such works as *Reisebriefe aus dem Süden* (1887), *Ethik der Volksherrschaft in Amerika* (1887), and *Ein Blick in den amerikanischen Dichterwald*. His German version of Longfellow's *Evangeline* in 1879 is perhaps the most widely known of his translations.

[18] Henny Koch (1854-1925) was particularly active as a writer of short stories from 1899 to her death.

[19] Vol. VIII of the series.

this work. Previous attempts at translation[20] had apparently been made, but almost insurmountable difficulties were encountered in reproducing the various passages in dialect. To paraphrase these was found equally unsatisfactory, since the dialects in themselves identify the character groups.

It is interesting to note that the translations of *The Prince and the Pauper* were made by women, who may have been particularly attracted to the work by the nature of the subject matter. Josephine Flach, a Catholic novelist of considerable repute, offered the first translation in 1887, and it was then published by the Verlag der "Deutschen Heimat" in Constance as *Fürst und Bettler*. The second translation appeared in 1890 under the title *Der Prinz und der Betteljunge. Eine Erzählung für die Jugend jeden Alters und Geschlechts*. Aside from the excellent translation by Helene Lobedan,[21] the work is interesting because of the 156 illustrations which accompany the text.

For the critical reaction to Mark Twain in these early years, we are dependent primarily on the personal opinions of individual scholars as expressed in the reviews[22] which appeared in the *Magazin für die Literatur des Auslandes*. In some instances these followed shortly after the publication of the respective works, in others a brief period elapsed. On the whole, these reviews are both factual and critical. Although they deal with the author's works individually, collectively they afford us an interesting view of the attitude of the early German critics towards Mark Twain.

One of the first contemporary German critics to acknowledge the literary potentialities of Mark Twain was a leading Austrian.

[20] Cf. Anton E. Schönbach, "Über amerikanische Romandichtung der Gegenwart," *Deutsche Rundschau*, XLVI (March, 1886), 422.

[21] Helene Lobedan (1839-1915) was active in translating novels of Edwards, Yates, Trollope, Cooper, Mancini, Dickens, Thackeray, Kingsley, Cherbuliez, Ohnet, Nesbit, and Mark Twain.

[22] Practically all the reviews appeared in *MfdLdA*. It was not until the end of the early period that such scholarly journals as *Archiv für das Studium der neueren Sprachen* and *Anglia: Beiblatt*, took an interest in Mark Twain. These reviews are supplemented by articles in various literary journals. These took no note of Mark Twain until 1886, when the *Deutsche Rundschau* (a scientific and literary as well as political journal) published an important discussion of the contemporary American novel by Anton E. Schönbach. Such journals as the *Gegenwart, Gesellschaft*, and *Illustrierte Zeitung*, though exhibiting a transitory interest in individual articles, refrained from any extended discussion of Mark Twain.

literary historian, Anton Emanuel Schönbach. Schönbach entered upon his academic career at the University of Graz in 1872, and shortly thereafter he began an extensive investigation of the political history of the United States. He undertook studies in American literature, particularly one of Emerson, and familiarized himself with contemporary American prose writings. In the succeeding years he attained distinction as a scholar and writer who through his ability to interest readers in the subject under discussion, exerted a wide literary influence.[23] As early as February of 1875 Schönbach delivered a series of three public lectures[24] at the Styrian university on the humorous prose of the Nineteenth Century. He restricted himself to the humoristic prose of England, Germany, and America, a procedure which he defended on the ground that humor is the unique domain of the Germanic mind. In the course of his third lecture he traced American humor in the prose works of the older romantic school of Cooper, Washington Irving, and Poe, and followed this with a discriminating analysis of the works of the contemporary American humorists, Thomas Bailey Aldrich, Mark Twain, and Bret Harte.

Although Schönbach accords Mark Twain the fullest measure of critical attention, he nevertheless relegates him to a subordinate position in the field of humorists. Bret Harte,[25] it seems to him at

[23] In 1888 Schönbach published a series of essays entitled *Über Lesen und Bildung* (Graz: Leuschner & Lubensky's, Universitäts-Buchhandlung, 1888). A special feature of this volume was the supplementary list of books which he himself compiled and which he personally recommended as a sort of literary guide for the German reader. Among the American writers of fiction he listed such authors as Alcott, Aldrich, Bret Harte, Cooper, Harris, Holmes, Howells, Irving, and Mark Twain. Of the latter's works he mentions specifically *Roughing It, Life on the Mississippi, The Adventures of Tom Sawyer,* and *The Innocents Abroad.* Inasmuch as Schönbach's work enjoyed considerable circulation, it is reasonable to assume that he assisted in directing the attention of many readers to Mark Twain.

[24] These lectures were delivered on the 15th, 16th, and 17th of February, 1875, in behalf of the fund for the widows of the "Steiermärkischen Schriftstellervereines." They appeared in book form shortly after under the title *Über die humoristische Prosa des XIX. Jahrhunderts* (Graz: Leuschner & Lubensky, 1875).

[25] It may be well to anticipate here the frequent comparison of Mark Twain and Bret Harte. Wilhelm Lange (*supra,* note 7), in his preface to a translation of Mark Twain's sketches in 1878, characterizes both as "Kinder der Sierra," but he stresses this distinction: Bret Harte, he says, conceives his material as a poet and fashions it into "ergreifende und stimmungsvolle Seelengemälde und Naturbilder," while Mark Twain approaches his material as a humorist and satirist—not a satirist in the sense of a superior scoffer without any trace of sympathy, but as an honest

the moment, far surpasses Mark Twain both as poet and prose-writer, for the work of Bret Harte suggests the "Dichter," while that of Mark Twain bears the stamp of a journalist or a good criminologist. This quality he finds particularly in the short essays and sketches, which he characterizes as Mark Twain's most effective work. The effect of these pithy impromptus he attributes to their striking originality and their humorous method of presenting material. Mark Twain, he contends, possesses an uncanny imaginative power for devising characters and situations, and this is enhanced and supplemented by an enviable ability to dramatize them as a most exquisite product of humor, but a humor based on exaggeration. Thus the national fame of the story of the *Jumping Frog,* to take merely one example, Schönbach asserts is due not so much to the story itself, which in his opinion offers nothing exactly unusual, but to the manner in which the story is related by Simon Wheeler. Nowhere else has the humorist given such striking expression to his consummate descriptive talent.

With equal incisiveness Schönbach analyzes the strength and weakness of Mark Twain's style. On the one hand, he finds it "remarkably expressive, clear, and plastic," original as the content itself, but far more artistic; on the other hand, he feels it lacks a certain polish and refinement. The classics might have given him the elegance and finish of an experienced and highly trained writer; but life and journalism were the really formative forces that influenced his style. These infused it with such power and vigor that one rarely is conscious of a lack of smoothness.

Schönbach's more or less favorable appraisal of Mark Twain does not extend to *The Innocents Abroad.* This work had been enthusiastically received in America, and its abundant popularity had been attested by the unusually large circulation in this country. The impression on the Continent, however, was less favorable. In

---

critic of social conditions who does not mince words to convey his satire effectively. Rudolf Doehn, political and literary critic, attributes the same basic principle to the art of both authors, the principle of depicting everyday life with its specific color. Both, he finds, attempt to prove that the most corrupt individual, regardless of his position in life, possesses in his heart a natural tendency toward good, a manifestation of sympathy, even though it be superficial and transitory. See Rudolf Doehn, *Aus dem amerikanischen Dichterwald* (Leipsic: Verlag von Otto Wigand, 1881), p. 140.

Germany it met with a rather cool reception. One may ascribe this, as Schönbach seems inclined to do,[26] either to the keen disappointment of the German reader with the substance and literary quality of the work or to the German's fundamental national conception of humor, which made it rather difficult for a German reader to understand the source of Mark Twain's humor. He misjudged the work in that he interpreted seriously the expressions of exaggerated national feeling, expressions which Schönbach calls "nur persiflierend." Among the early German critics who reviewed *The Innocents Abroad* there is an interesting contrast of reactions. Schönbach seems to have been one of comparatively few who were able to find some entertainment in the humorous presentation of the tourist's personal adventures and his reactions to the customs of the lands he visited. Dr. Friedmann[27] has a similar experience, in spite of the fact that he strongly disapproves of European trips for specifically literary purposes. On the other hand, Eduard Engel, the editor of the *Magazin für die Literatur des Auslandes* from 1879 to 1883, and a writer of distinction, is sharply critical. He rejects the explanation, advanced by Schönbach and supported by Friedmann, that Mark Twain is merely joking.[28] Mark Twain's propensity to ridicule works of art, Engel contends bitterly, is not the culmination of modern American humor as some American newspapers and reviews might suggest, but rather a visible expression of the author's "Iroquoian ignorance" and of the characteristically American lack of reverence for those things which the European regards as glorious treasures of civilization. If Mark Twain had been able to follow the dictates of his own richly endowed nature, if he had not made the glaring error of yielding to the "taste" of the American newspaper reader, his *The Innocents Abroad* might have become a "permanent masterpiece of Anglo-Saxon humor." But in its present form Engel finds it a book which merely provokes one's anger. He is, in fact, exasperated that a member of the literary guild should venture to perpetrate such "monstrous crudities" in a work which contains examples of the most original humor, such as seldom occur even in the works

[26] Schönbach, *op. cit.*, p. 79.
[27] *MfdLdA, April* 29, 1876, p. 262.
[28] *MfdLdA,* October 9, 1880, p. 576.

of a Dickens. He cannot, inferentially, conceal a feeling of regret that Mark Twain made himself immortally ludicrous. A book of travel, he declares, should be purely informational and therefore should not attempt a psychological criticism of a country and its people. Such works as the *Reisebücher* of Bädeker, Meyer, and Murray are valid and defensible because they adhere to their original purpose. But Mark Twain in *The Innocents Abroad* consciously deviates from the accepted pattern of books of travel. Utterly heedless of the sensibilities of others, he attempts a humorously critical evaluation of a foreign people and its civilization; the very effort to do this reflects a uniquely brazen and offensive attitude. In view of such an antipathy to Mark Twain's work, Engel's conclusion that "if the muses wish Mark Twain well, they will never permit him to cross the Atlantic again," does not surprise us.

On the publication of *A Tramp Abroad* and its humorous descriptions of a trip through Germany and Switzerland, Engel[29] is pleased to note marked progress in Mark Twain's art. He observes with considerable satisfaction that the crudeness which at times almost reached the level of actual vulgarity in *The Innocents Abroad*, occurs less frequently and not in such solid dimensions. Passages in which the author's good-natured humor asserts itself, he finds more numerous and better distributed; in fact, Mark Twain's humor occasionally becomes so subtle that the average individual is not able to detect it. The German reader, it seems to him, will confine his attention principally to those portions of the book which are German in their subject-matter. Especially "The Awful German Language" with its admixture of ignorance, good-nature, and wit he acknowledges and recommends ungrudgingly as "das stärkste, was Mark Twain je geleistet." It must be said to Engel's credit that in spite of his condemnation of Mark Twain's art as expressed in *The Innocents Abroad*, he now shows himself ready to revise his judgment. Although he is not fully reconciled to the author's procedure, he nevertheless does not undervalue his achievement. He is sufficiently impressed to agree with Schönbach that Mark Twain is capable of more mature works. But

[29] *Ibid.*, p. 578.

he reiterates his conviction that he should remain in America and apply his humor to the judgment of conditions he understands. Then the German reader will pardon such adolescent sins as *The Innocents Abroad*.

In contrast to his almost scathing denunciation of *The Innocents Abroad*, Engel's reaction[30] to *Roughing It* is favorable. He is glad to give it his unstinted approval, which he intends as an instructive commentary on, and a counter-critique to, his adverse criticism of *The Innocents Abroad. Roughing It*, he points out, is distinctive because it is a realistic reproduction of personal experiences in the Far West and in the silver-mines of Nevada that is American to the core, rooted in native soil, and saturated with a specific local color. Friedmann[31] likewise recognizes the unique quality of the work, and he, as well as Schönbach,[32] assigns an even greater value to it than Engel does. The picturesque and lively accounts of frontier experiences, he contends, actually constitute a *Kulturskizze* of unquestionable value.

The German critics, however, are as yet far from recognizing the singular value and the artistic merit of *The Adventures of Tom Sawyer* and *The Adventures of Huckleberry Finn*, even though their observations suggest a somewhat vague premonition of the real quality of these works. Schönbach does not underestimate the value of the former as a work of fiction. He readily concedes that the author's unusual comprehension and skillful portrayal of the "boy-world,"[33] with its freedom of action and conduct and its early development of independence, self-reliance, and responsibility, gives the narrative such a sustained interest as to make it "a decided success."[34] Nevertheless he subordinates it in merit to such works as *Tom Brown's Schooldays* and Aldrich's *Story of a Bad Boy*. Engel, on the other hand, is inclined to be more enthusiastic about *Tom Sawyer* and to rate it consider-

[30] *MfdLdA*, November 27, 1880, p. 681.

[31] *MfdLdA*, April 22, 1876, p. 242.

[32] *Deutsche Rundschau*, XLVI, 431, henceforth cited as *DR*.

[33] Schönbach admits the superior skill of American writers in the delineation of the boy-mind. He attributes that particularly to the fact that American children and the American conception of family-life provide the most suitable material for such a universal study of boyhood.

[34] *DR*, XLVI, 429.

ably higher.[35] He compares it favorably with Miss Alcott's *Little Women,* and places it on a par with Aldrich's *Story of a Bad Boy* and with the best creative work of Bret Harte. In imaginative power he goes so far as to contrast it with the finished productions of a Marryat and a Cooper. He, too, is so impressed with the charm and universality of the instructive picture of the "boy-conscience" that he finds it utterly incomprehensible that Mark Twain is known as the author of *The Innocents Abroad* rather than of *Tom Sawyer.* In regard to *The Adventures of Huckleberry Finn,* one encounters a surprising lack of sympathetic understanding of those human qualities which constitute the "large feature" of the work. Schönbach, one of those most competent in the literature of America, contents himself with merely giving a *résumé* of the content. His actual criticism is limited to the following: "We discover no new traits in the characters of the young heroes; only Huck's figure is fuller and his inventive power reveals itself in difficult situations."[36] Engel, still faithfully contributing reviews of Mark Twain's works, apparently considered this one of such little importance that he withheld his personal reaction. In his *Geschichte der Literatur Nordamerikas,*[37] in which he seeks to define Mark Twain's place in the literature of America, he disregards the work completely. Contrasted with the marked indifference of these two prominent critics, the unqualified approval of Henny Koch, the translator of the work, merits serious attention. Among German critics, in fact, Fräulein Koch appears to be the only one to give *Huckleberry Finn* a finely intelligent appreciation. In the publisher's preface to the German translation she attempts to explain its irresistible appeal. The realistic portrayal of the principal characters in their primitive, native state, the wholesome agreeable humor, the moral struggle within Huck's own heart and conscience, the picture of slavery as an accepted and sanctioned institution, and the very sound, moral tone which never offends our deepest and most reverent feelings, these con-

[35] Cf. note 28 above.
[36] *DR,* XLVI, 430.
[37] As an appendix to his *Geschichte der englischen Literatur,* 8th ed. (Leipsic: Brandstetter, 1915).

stitute, she declares, the vital elements that sustain and enhance the reader's interest.

With the appearance of each new volume, the German critics are frankly astonished at Mark Twain's widely diversified approach. In practically each instance they are able to catalogue the genre of the volume as a collection of sketches, a book of travel, or fiction. The publication of *The Prince and the Pauper,* however, placed them in a quandary. Here was a work that apparently defied critical classification. The immediate impulse was to term it a "historical romance." Though they find this new product difficult to appraise, the critics nevertheless are agreed on one point: that Mark Twain's experiment is an utter failure. Engel[38] confesses his delight in the attempted hoax on history and the historical novel, yet he contends that "historical romance" would be a misnomer, since historical truth and the objectivity of the author are flagrantly disregarded. History, he points out, offered no such episode as presented in *The Prince and the Pauper;* it only suggested a very suitable subject for an embellishing imagination. Mark Twain in this instance uses the historical characters merely as external supports for his imaginative pictures. Engel, however, does not commit himself definitely in regard to the accuracy of Mark Twain's assumptions. That decision he leaves to the future. Turning to his treatment of the historical material, Engel is quite convinced not only that Europeans, who stand in such reverent awe of the past and harbor such an aversion to the present, resent the American's new procedure, but also that no one in Europe would have ventured such a reckless artistic reworking of the historical past. To prove his point, he reminds us that Goethe in his *Egmont* and Schiller in the delineation of such characters as Thekla, Posa, Don Carlos, Joan, and William Tell used historical material in such a way as to satisfy their own artistic needs. Whether a poet, he argues, for his own artistic purposes goes only so far as to ennoble the Infant Carlos or to restore Maria Stuart's youth, or whether he completely invents an occurrence of the greatest moment, as, for instance, the *Vertauschung*

[38] *MfdLdA,* May 6, 1882, pp. 259 f.

of Prince Edward and Tom Canty in Mark Twain's work, that is only a quantitative distinction. Such a procedure on the part of the author is justified and incontestable. Literary critics[39] may indeed condemn such an approach, but the average reader will not be concerned with the author's attitude toward history and his treatment of it. He will react to the appeal to the "eternally youthful" within him. That leads Engel to the conclusion that the work will soon become one of the most popular juvenile books, especially in England, and he finds it amusing to observe how this book might alter the historical conception of the life of Edward VI in the minds of thousands of English citizens. Nevertheless, he does not consider it a work of permanent literary value. At most, it is very entertaining reading, even in times of trouble. "Ein Buch zum Gesundlachen" perhaps characterizes it most effectively.

The Innocents Abroad and A Tramp Abroad had left with many a German reader the impression that Mark Twain was above all an author of books of travel. The Adventures of Tom Sawyer and The Prince and the Pauper, then, assisted in partially dispelling that impression and replacing it with a far more acceptable portrait of Mark Twain as an author of juvenile books. At the same time there was a growing crystallization of thoughtful opinion that Mark Twain was a writer of literary importance. There can be no doubt that Life on the Mississippi did much to confirm and to solidify this opinion. The reception accorded this "Odyssey of the Mississippi" was, on the whole, favorable. Schönbach, for example, is inclined to rank it as the author's best, and it is highly probable that many a German reader endorsed this view. Though other German critics may differ with Schönbach on the rating of the work, there is in one respect a decided unanimity of opinion. Without exception, they emphasize the deep significance of the author's own life and experience for his poetic presentations and the cultural value inherent in the descriptions of life along the Mississippi. Adolf Stern,[40] literary historian and

---

[39] Schönbach thoroughly disapproves of The Prince and the Pauper. The enlargement of the material, he contends, destroys the naïveté, the principal attraction of such narratives, and he finds the work totally devoid of the imaginative tone which is necessary to give charm to such an invention (DR, XLVI, 432).

[40] His reputation as an author of rank rests primarily on his work, Johannes Gutenberg (1872), and on his various collections of Novellen (1863-1879).

biographer of Otto Ludwig, in particular attaches the utmost importance to the work as a reflection of the spirit of rugged individualism in American life.[41]

Although the general tone of the scant critical response to *A Connecticut Yankee in King Arthur's Court* is favorable, the substance of it is disappointing and not very illuminating. Reviews were contributed by the Jewish novelist and critic, Max Osterburg-Verakoff,[42] and by two of the outstanding Anglists of the day, Richard Wülker[43] and Julius Zupitza.[44] These critics are in substantial agreement in stressing imagination and humor as the two dominant characteristics of a work, the fascination and appeal of which is augmented by the author's vitality and originality. There is, however, a difference in interpretation. Zupitza finds the essence of humor in the work in the abundant contrasts that arise from the conflict between the modern and the medieval-romantic.[45] Wülker, on the other hand, dismisses the matter with the cryptic remark that Mark Twain's humor is too well known to require comment;[46] but he does observe that the author would have gained immeasurably if he had curbed his tendency toward the burlesque. It is particularly with this latter view that Osterberg-Verakoff differs. He, too, emphasizes the rare combination of humor and imagination, but he defends the free play of the author's fancy.[47] In view of the distinguished literary and editorial experience of

[41] *Das Magazin*, March 30, 1889, p. 213.

[42] He was also editor of the journal *Süddeutsche Literaturschau*. Numbered among his works are the stage dramas *Eine Verschwörung* (1886) and *Kunst und Leben* (1887), the novel *Himmlische Liebe* (1889), *20 Tage durch Chicago* (1892), and *Allgemeines über das Stuttgarter Hoftheater* (1896).

[43] Wülker was born in 1845, and was professor in the University of Leipsic at the time of his death in 1910. Together with M. Trautmann he established the journal *Anglia*, which he edited to 1890. He is particularly remembered as the author of the extensive *Grundriss zur Geschichte der angelsächsischen Literatur* (1885) and the *Geschichte der englischen Literatur* (1896).

[44] Zupitza (1844-1895) was professor of English philology in the University of Berlin. He is widely known for innumerable studies in philology, the most important of which are said to be *Einführung in das Studium des Mittelhochdeutschen* (1868), an Old English *Übungsbuch* (1874), and various editions of Middle English and Old English works. From 1890 to 1895 he was editor of the *Archiv für das Studium der neueren Sprachen*. Two years before his death he was made an honorary member of the Modern Language Association of America.

[45] *Archiv für das Studium der neueren Sprachen*, LXXXV, 101.

[46] *Anglia: Beiblatt*, II (April 1, 1891), 11.

[47] *Die Gesellschaft*, October 1890, pp. 1549 f.

these professorial critics, one would have expected greater breadth of treatment and more critical insight. Their attitude toward the work is cordial, but reserved. There seems to be justification for Osterberg-Verakoff's remark that many critics and readers accepted the signature of Mark Twain as a sufficient guarantee of the character and quality of a work without feeling the necessity for any further evaluation.

The limited references to Mark Twain in the histories of literature in these years were not calculated greatly to enhance his prestige. At best they corroborate the favorable comments of contemporary critics, and strengthen the impression that in some circles at least he was being recognized as a literary figure, even though only as a humorist. Whether these literary histories furthered Mark Twain and his work in Germany is a matter of speculation. In the fifth edition (1875) of his *Illustrierte Geschichte der Weltliteratur* (which originally appeared in 1851) Johannes Scherr, German literary historian and novelist,[48] does not mention Mark Twain. This should not, however, occasion surprise, for Mark Twain was just then being introduced into Germany by the Grunow firm in Leipsic. But evidence of a growing acquaintance with his work appears in Scherr's sixth edition (1880), which contains this important addition: "In the narratives and descriptions of Mark Twain the humorous conception of man and the world likewise comes to the fore."[49] In 1881 Rudolf Doehn[50] published a series of literary-historical sketches in which he attempted "to formulate a chronological history of American

---

[48] Scherr (1817-1886) spent the greater part of his life in Switzerland, whither he had been forced to flee in 1849 for political reasons. From 1860 he was professor of history in the Polytechnical Institute in Zürich. Aside from his literary and cultural histories, *Deutsche Kultur- und Sittengeschichte* (3 vols., 1852/53), *Allgemeine Geschichte der Literatur* (2 vols., 1851), and *Geschichte der Religion* (3 vols., 1855-1857), Scherr also wrote some purely humorous sketches, the most interesting of which is *Rosi Zurflüh* (1860), and the *Novellenbuch,* a collection of novellettes (10 vols., 1873-1877). His vivid style, his vehement bias, and his biting wit caused many critics to compare him with Carlyle.

[49] P. 119.

[50] Doehn spent almost twelve years in the United States as author, soldier, and legislator in the state of Missouri. The knowledge gained from this experience qualified him to undertake literary and political studies. Of a political nature are *Die politischen Parteien in den Vereinigten Staaten* and *Die Administrationen der Präsidenten U. S. Grant und R. B. Hayes*.

literature" under the title *Aus dem amerikanischen Dichterwald*.[51] On the whole Doehn re-echoes the opinions of Schönbach but supplements these with brief references to *Tom Sawyer*, "the eminently successful boys' story," and to *The Gilded Age*, "a satirical criticism of speculative mania, political intrigue, and corruption." *A Tramp Abroad* and *Life on the Mississippi*, however, are passed by in silence. It is probable that Doehn's work was little known and without influence on the reading public. On the other hand, it is more than probable that Eduard Engel's history of American literature, with its decidedly sympathetic approach, was an important contribution to the spread of knowledge concerning Mark Twain and his work. In 1883 Engel added an appendix on American literature to his *Geschichte der englischen Literatur*. Later this was published separately as *Geschichte der Literatur Nordamerikas*.[52] Engel incorporates practically the same ideas into this work which he had expressed in his reviews, except that he is now more favorably inclined towards *The Innocents Abroad*. This is particularly reflected in his strenuous objection to "an eminent German literary historian's" evaluation of Mark Twain as a "Hanswurst" or a "wütender Deutschenfresser."[53] With Engel there is now, as contrasted with his early marked antipathy to Mark Twain, a disposition to extoll him along with American humorists in general. Such characterizations as "a benefactor of mankind" or "a kind gift of compassionate heaven"[54] evidence a decided change in attitude and reflect perhaps a rising enthusiasm for Mark Twain on the part of certain circles of German readers.

Again, it is problematical whether Gustav Körting's[55] *Grundriss der Geschichte der englischen Literatur*[56] played any part in directing attention to Mark Twain. He interprets English literature in the narrow sense of the word, but includes the literature of

[51] Leipsic: Verlag von Otto Wigand, 1881.

[52] Leipsic: Wilhelm Friedrich. (No date.)

[53] Engel surmises this remark applies only to *A Tramp Abroad*. On the contrary, this work, he feels, gives concrete evidence that Mark Twain was a "friend" of Germany.

[54] *Op. cit.*, p. 51.

[55] Körting (1845-1913) was professor of Romance and English philology in the "Königliche Akademie" in Münster. His *Handbuch der romanischen Philologie* appeared in 1896 after he had removed to the University in Kiel.

[56] Münster i.W.: Schöningh, 1887.

North America to the extent of commenting in brief footnotes on the most important American authors. For further information he refers the German reader to the Tauchnitz Catalogue. His critical comment includes a few remarks on Mark Twain as the author of numerous humorous short stories and sketches. The humor of the earlier works he finds fresh and within reasonable bounds, while that of the later appears frequently quite forced. That and a few lines regarding Mark Twain's life is the extent of Körting's contribution.[57] F. P. Bierbaum's[58] *History of the English Language and Literature from the Earliest Times until the Present Day, including the American Literature*[59] can hardly be said to have had a wide circulation. Yet it is of some importance in that it indicates the trend of German literary histories. He, too, merely devotes a few lines to our American humorist. As a "humorous novel-writer" he is "a prolific writer, whose humor, mixed with a fair dose of satire, chiefly consists in hyperbolical presentations. *Innocents Abroad, A Tramp Abroad,* and *The Prince and the Pauper,* a pathetic, not humorous story, are the most popular of his writings."[60] It is also extremely doubtful whether Karl Knortz'[61] comprehensive *Geschichte der nordamerikanischen Literatur,*[62] regarded by some responsible critics as one of the most accurate and exhaustive of all histories of American literature in Germany, played more than a minor rôle in popularizing Mark Twain. In common with the other literary historians of these years, Knortz withholds extended comment. The greater part of the one-and-a-half page appraisal merely acquaints the reader with certain vital biographical facts, while the more critical portion characterizes Mark Twain as a keen observer, whose humor, wit, satire, and sarcasm seem to find expression only on his trips to foreign lands. Though Knortz lauds the originality and

[57] *Op. cit.*, p. 385, note 3.
[58] Bierbaum was professor at the Girls' High School in Karlsruhe.
[59] 2nd ed.; Heidelberg: Weiss, 1889.
[60] *Ibid.*, p. 249.
[61] Knortz, a German-American author and educator, had done much to arouse interest in American literature through his translations of American poets and his literary essays on American legends, capitalism, and labor. Prior to 1891 he published *Longfellow: literar-historische Studie* (1879), *Walt Whitman, ein Vortrag* (1886), and *Humoristische Gedichte* (1889).
[62] 2 v. Berlin: Hans Lüstenöder, 1891.

the naïveté of the American's wit, he does not fail to express his displeasure with Mark Twain's contemptuously hilarious approach to the language, customs, and music of Germany.[63]

It is obvious from the foregoing analyses that humor was the one characteristic which German opinion at this time associated with Mark Twain's art. In almost every instance it is recognized, but no attempt is made to analyze it. One might explain this indifference on the ground that Mark Twain did not illustrate an æsthetic or literary theory that came into contact with contemporary movements in Germany, nor represent any school which the German critics felt constrained to attack. His field of literary endeavor, the field of humor, was presumably so far removed from the German horizon at the moment that the German mind simply lacked the capacity to understand it. It is not until the year 1886 that we meet with a few isolated cases in which critics inquire into the origin of his humor. Mark Twain's humor, they all agree, is to be identified, not with the humor that was inherited[64] from England, Scotland, and Ireland, but with the "American humor" that developed independently of Europe and found expression in the newspapers.[65] For, in the opinion of Ludwig Salomon,[66] author and journalist, it was the contemporary American newspaper with its columns of brief humorous narratives, anecdotes, and pungent descriptions of common daily occurrences, that partially satisfied the intense desire of the materialistically inclined American for refreshing humor as a mental stimulus and a means of revitalizing energy.

With the American newspaper as the basic source for their

---

[63] Knortz, op. cit., II, 459.

[64] Hermann Kindt (*Die Gegenwart*, XXX, 53) contends that the humor not only of the incomparable Washington Irving but also of such authors as Sam Slick (Judge Halliburton) in his *Clockmaker,* James Russell Lowell (the excellent connoisseur of German and Italian literature) in his *Biglow Papers,* Oliver Wendell Holmes in his *Autocrat,* and Charles G. Leland in his Hans Breitmann poetry, is characteristic of the mother countries—England, Scotland, and Ireland with its "Irish Bulls"—and therefore cannot be considered as truly representative of "American humor."

[65] This humor is accordingly called "newspaper humor" or "broad humor."

[66] Salomon (1844-1911) was highly admired for his comprehensive reading and moderated judgment. In the opinion of leading critics, he will long be remembered as the deserving "Geschichtschreiber des deutschen Zeitungswesens" and as the author of a *Deutsche Nationalliteratur des 19. Jahrhunderts.*

analyses, our critics then seek to determine the fundamental characteristics of American humor. One searches in vain, however, for a clear definition. Apparently recognizing the difficulty of defining the subject, they avoid saying what it essentially is and restrict themselves to "giving instances without theories." Among the most common elements prevalent in American humor Salomon,[67] without critical elaboration, enumerates amusement, entertainment, gross exaggeration, grotesque extravaganza, and insolent swagger. To these Kindt[68] adds a certain amiable naïveté and originality of feeling, and Engel[69] an unbelievable objectivity and seriousness. Exaggeration, which Schönbach[70] characterizes as merely the tendency to express one's self strongly and vigorously, is generally accepted by the German critics as the foremost ingredient of American humor. This appears in the inclination to select words with a stronger connotation than that of the so-called "refined English." It is only natural that our critics should attempt to measure American humor by the standard of German humor; the obvious purpose, of course, is to emphasize the deficiencies of the former. Salomon,[71] for example, comes to the conclusion that American humor, in contrast to German humor, contains nothing of the melancholy resignation of a Jean Paul or a Wilhelm Raabe, and nothing of the depth of thought of a Friedrich Vischer. Engel,[72] on the other hand, stresses the fact that German humor is to a great extent synonymous with sentimentality. It carries with it "etwas Feuchtes." Dickens, he explains, owed the great popularity he enjoyed among the German people to this element in his work. American humor, however, which is frequently characterized as a "dry" humor, lacks the very quality that is so appealing to the German nature. The feeling that all the essential elements of American humor find characteristic and striking expression in Mark Twain, leads German critics in this early period without exception to label him as the best representative of American humor. There is a marked tendency to identify

[67] *Illustrierte Zeitung,* October 6, 1888, p. 345.
[68] *Die Gegenwart,* XXX, 53
[69] *Op. cit.,* p. 51.
[70] *DR,* XLVI, 427.
[71] Cf. note 67 above.
[72] *Op. cit.,* p. 50.

American humor almost exclusively with Mark Twain, who, they note, contributed to its development by enlarging the fundamental character of humor with a certain drastic sharpness which develops at times into biting satire.

On the basis of the foregoing one must admit that the body of critical opinion is as yet quite small. Yet in spite of its inadequacy, it is possible to draw some definite conclusions regarding Mark Twain's acceptability in Germany. On the whole, one may say that his works enjoyed a favorable initial reception at the hands of both the public and the critics. With very few exceptions, each year brought the publication of one or more volumes. It may not be an important criterion of German taste for Mark Twain's works, but it is worthy of note that many of his works appeared in Germany in the original or in translation shortly after their publication in the United States.

The publications in Germany in these early years were of sufficient number and scope to impress the critics profoundly with the author's extraordinary versatility. Experiences in journalism, river piloting, mining, and exploration, "not only in their results, but also in their processes," all found expression in these works to such an extent that the German commentators in general interpret them as an adequate reflection of the author's own varied and interesting career. Although none of his books presents the composite of a great life, such as we find in Goethe's *Faust,* each, with very few exceptions, represents a chapter in his life. Not free formation according to the laws of art, but the concentrated reproduction of an interesting life is the domain of his creation.

Mark Twain's position as a story-teller, the critics point out, is determined by the development of his life. Just as his briefer writings still have the form of humorous newspaper articles or readings, so his larger works reveal the talent of an able paragraphist and reporter. From the very beginning of his activity he saw in his public the newspaper reader whose attention he had to excite and retain with strong stimulants. Satisfactory evidence of this is found in the sketches, where one jest follows another, where seriousness alternates with farce, and pathos with humor in pungent but also in grotesque contrast.

Mark Twain's humor, the critics stress, had its origin in the contemporary American journals and newspapers. It is based on exaggeration, but an exaggeration suggested by a studied naïveté, a dry objectivity, an affected touch of irreverence, and above all, by a biting satire.

There is no doubt that Mark Twain had begun to make a forceful impression on German critics. There is a disposition to refer to him as "a remarkably independent and original observer," "a thinker," and "an honest critic," and also at least one instance where he is called "the greatest American humorist." This is exceptional, and a questioning and even hostile attitude also appears; but the opinion gradually emerges that he is a literary personality of importance and one worthy of continued interest. The conviction also grows that he is a serious writer with decided potentialities to do work of a more ambitious kind.

II

EXTENSION OF MARK TWAIN'S PRESTIGE
1892-1904

First "Gesamt-Ausgabe" (Lutz)——Michael Georg Conrad——Sintenis——
Introduction into schools——Fischer——Illustrated edition——"Eisenbahn-
Ausgabe" (Lutz)——*Neue Folge*——von Thaler——Wurm——Summary.

The years that followed witnessed a steady growth of public interest in Mark Twain. The frequent reprints of the works already published and the steadily mounting number of additional works, which were just as varied in form and subject matter as those of earlier years, consolidated and strengthened the favorable initial impression in Germany, and enlarged, in some measure at least, his reading public. The year 1892, in fact, marks the initial stage of an extraordinary activity on behalf of Mark Twain. Disregarding the rather discouraging reception of his "Stern-banner-Serie,"[1] Robert Lutz, the young journalist and publisher, with his appreciation of the distinct and individual character of Mark Twain's humor still undimmed, resolved to capitalize on the very favorable public response to Mark Twain's second visit to Germany and Switzerland in June of the preceding year. We may well ascribe a great importance to this second visit.[2] Mark Twain was now a distinguished man of letters, recognized and saluted wherever he went. At diplomatic functions he was always a welcome guest. His social life during the months in Berlin was such as to bring him into contact with the most prominent men and women of all walks of life.[3] Whether the attending publicity had a favorable effect on the sale of his books is a matter of conjecture. Certainly it is not unreasonable to assume that it made his name widely known among all classes of the German people. Lutz recognized the value of this advertising and redoubled his efforts to popularize Mark Twain's books. He now undertook to

---

[1] *Supra*, pp. 12-14. In spite of the fact that he had arranged for only a comparatively small edition of some 2500 copies of each volume, Lutz experienced considerable difficulty in disposing of the edition. Only in the case of the three Mark Twain volumes did his efforts meet with encouraging results.

[2] Cf. Chapter I, n. 12.

[3] Paine, *op. cit.*, III, 921-944; 949-952.

publish, first in serial form, a reliable six-volume edition of *Mark Twains ausgewählte humoristische Schriften.*[4] This edition was advertised as the first German "Gesamt-Ausgabe seiner besten humoristischen Schriften." Vol. I contained *Tom Sawyers Streiche und Abenteuer;* Vol. II, *Abenteuer und Fahrten des Huckleberry Finn;* Vol. III, *Skizzenbuch;* Vol. IV, *Auf dem Mississippi. Lehr- und Wanderjahre. Nach dem fernen Westen;* Vol. V, *Im Gold- und Silberlande. Lehr- und Wanderjahre;* and Vol. VI, *Reisebilder* and a short history of the author's life. Critics have called attention to the significance of the fact that the edition began with the two youthful autobiographical books and not with the volume of sketches which at that time were by far the more popular.

The work of selection demanded the utmost care. Whatever pertained exclusively to local conditions or treated specifically of situations and events which no longer had a sufficient historical interest for the German reader had to be eliminated.[5] The result was an edition which, through the judicious grouping of the works, attained its principal objective of mirroring the close relationship between the author's life and his creations.

The critical reaction to this edition, however, was not uniformly favorable. An anonymous reviewer writing in the *Beilage zur Allgemeinen Zeitung* (Munich) several years later[6] has nothing but words of praise for the American humorist. He reaffirms in general terms the opinions of the large section of German criticism which adjudged Mark Twain first of all as a humorist and then as a satirist. Only in one respect do we notice a new note: he is

---

[4] Lutz' efforts to gain proper recognition for Mark Twain's works in wider circles were also shared by other publishers. Tauchnitz published an English edition of *The American Claimant* in 1892, one volume of *Sketches* in 1893, and one volume of *Tom Sawyer Abroad* in 1894. Shortly after the appearance of the Tauchnitz edition of *The American Claimant,* the Deutsche Verlagsanstalt of Stuttgart issued a German translation of this work under the title *Der amerikanische Prätendent.* Important also is Reclam, who had been particularly active in the publication of cheap editions of Mark Twain's sketches, for his fifth volume of some ninety-three pages of *Ausgewählte Skizzen.* These were translated by David Haek, Hungarian author of arabesques, sketches, and aphorisms. Widely circulated also was a volume of *Skizzen,* translated by H. Löwe, the editor of the humorous column of the *Berliner Lokal-Anzeiger,* and published in Meyer's Volksbücher of 1893.

[5] This explains why Mark Twain's extensive work *The Innocents Abroad* is represented in the collection by only a few of the most successful scenes and sketches.

[6] May 6, 1896.

the first of the critics to call specific attention to "the lively feeling for landscape" which reflects itself in all his works, and to appraise his books accordingly as "books which are adapted for out-of-door reading," as "genuine products of nature which demand a background of forest, mountain, and flowery field." On the other hand, the publication of this edition led Michael Georg Conrad to take an extreme position in his appraisal of Mark Twain's art.[7] Conrad (1846-1927) was one of the most important critics in the 1880's. In collaboration with Wolfgang Kirchbach he established the journal *Die Gesellschaft*, which, as the official organ of information and opinion in German Naturalism, set forth the principles of that movement. But the sphere of Conrad's intellectual interests had widened until there was hardly a field of modern life that he did not observe critically. Not only German literature but also foreign literature drew his critical attention. For years he had watched with growing restlessness the growth of Mark Twain's vogue in Germany, and had come to the conclusion that this could be explained only on the ground that the philistine world finds it fashionable to pay homage to a humorist. "Even if Mark Twain were to approach the German in a spirit of still greater disrespect than he considers proper both as an American and as an humorist," Conrad observes with ill-concealed irritation, "he would not suffer any appreciable loss in German opinion." Although he does not underestimate the value of humor in its own domain, Conrad administers in reserved but emphatic language a sharp rebuke to the German public for its enthusiastic reception of an American humorist in the face of its indifference towards a Heinrich Heine. Incidentally he compares Mark Twain's horizon with that of Julius Stinde in his well-known Buchholz series, and he denounces the presumptuousness of any attempt to associate him with a Dickens or a Jean Paul in depth of feeling. A consideration of these factors leads Conrad to pose what he regards as a question of especial pertinence: "What is Mark Twain's value as a spiritual force for the progress and advancement of culture?" He comes to the conclusion that "as a humanizing spiritual force Mark Twain is of as much value as a genial clown

[7] *Die Gesellschaft,* November, 1893, p. 1508.

of the circus," that "he represents no moral factor." However, this candid criticism is tempered somewhat by an acknowledgement of Mark Twain's distinction as a sharply humorous observer, a masterful delineator of the adventurous, and a keen judge of the human soul. In view of the fact that Conrad devotes practically three-fourths of his review to a *résumé* of some of the salient facts in Mark Twain's colorful life, one cannot escape the impression that he was not entirely immune to the universal enthusiasm for his personality.

Even though it cannot be substantiated by documentary references, it is quite possible that there were many German readers and critics who were interested in Conrad's conclusions and who, because of his influential position, accepted his appraisal of Mark Twain's literary value. On the other hand, there is evidence of an increasingly favorable attitude toward the American writer's achievements. Among the recognized authorities on American literature in Germany the name of Franz Sintenis, professor in the University of Dorpat, merits our consideration as a representative of this trend in German opinion in these years. In a very competent discussion,[8] Sintenis advances the thesis that Mark Twain's literary work should be identified as a living symbol of the spirit of an America that had shown its vitality and joy of life in the struggle for unification. In this connection he traces briefly but effectively the tremendous influence of certain factors in the development of America, such as the introduction of East Indian sugar cane in 1493, the invention of the cotton gin in 1793, the steady importation and influx of Negroes with the resulting problem of slavery, the conflict between the material advantages of slavery and moral scruples regarding the traffic in slaves, and the appeal to the entire Christian world in *Uncle Tom's Cabin*. But, he argues, inasmuch as North America has not reached the years of maturity in which the individual is as clearly conscious of his mental as of his physical powers, one can not with reasonable propriety expect to find the sterling accomplishments of a serious man. It would be far more appropriate to char-

---

[8] Sintenis, *Literarische Ansichten in Vorträgen* (Dorpat-Fellin: Karow's Universitätsbuchhandlung, 1894), pp. 60-76.

acterize Mark Twain as "an enterprising youth who has just begun to realize the seriousness of life, but while contemplating his future plans does not abandon his youthful pranks." To clarify this point of view, Sintenis instances short extracts, "six pictures of American life," from the author's various autobiographical works to explain the labyrinth of his development and by indirection, the peculiarities and limitations of his art.

Having enunciated his theory that Mark Twain's works are to be interpreted in the light of American history, Sintenis then proceeds to a consideration of the author's sketches—a matter of importance for our discussion in so far as they permit of a contrast with Bret Harte. The unmistakable similarities he lists are very limited in number and are to be found in such themes as the presentation of youthful dissimulation and force of will[9] or the humane defense of the Chinese against the brutal persecution of the Californians.[10] Although the attitude of the two writers towards the Negroes and the Indians reflects a similar humane spirit, their treatment of these classes shows little resemblance. The differences, on the other hand, are far more numerous and readily established. Sintenis directs attention primarily to certain dissimiliarities in subject-matter and technique which are especially noticeable on account of the compact and richly suggestive style of both writers. Bret Harte's sphere of influence, he points out, is restricted primarily to California, and only very seldom extends to the East; Mark Twain, on the other hand, encompasses the entire Union. Bret Harte is, in so far as his figures represent elements from all the world, a "local cosmopolite"; Mark Twain's horizon embraces the entire, unified nation and recognizes everywhere the Yankee. Bret Harte shows only how he has seen the world; Mark Twain, with a strongly didactic tone invariably colored by irony, draws conclusions from his philosophy of life which are directed toward immediate social reforms. In direct antithesis to the objective formality of Bret Harte, who imparts his own natural nobility and elegance even to reprobates, we have

[9] The parallel here concerns Mark Twain's official toast to the babies at a banquet in honor of General Grant and Bret Harte's *Ehrwürdige Betrüger*.

[10] As portrayed in Bret Harte's *Wan-Lee, the Pagan*, and Mark Twain's *Disgraceful Persecution of a Boy*.

the subjective humor and spirit of Mark Twain, who at times condescends to the level of the lowliest and not infrequently drags down with him even the highly respected, yet in doing so retains a persistent charm. In common with other German critics, Sintenis credits both authors with an exceptional decorum, and attributes much of their success to this quality. He acknowledges Bret Harte's literary excellence, but a comparison of their creative works compels him to assign to Mark Twain superiority in the creation of comprehensive works.[11] This recognition, however, is qualified by the observation that Mark Twain's artistic productions lack "the breath of the full culture" which would have given his amazing natural talents the consecration of a great writer. The marked absence of this supreme attribute is explained by the fact that life itself had trained him. It must be conceded that Sintenis struck a new note in the interpretation of Mark Twain, but there is no evidence that his views were widely circulated or that they were greatly instrumental in dissipating the popular conception of Mark Twain as merely a buffoon. It may be assumed that his influence was confined principally to intellectual circles with little or no effect on the masses.

There is some concrete evidence that Mark Twain was gaining a wider recognition in academic circles as a writer to be treated with seriousness and respect. Many of the educators in Germany, in direct repudiation of Conrad, came to realize that his works were artistically valuable in that they were representative of the life and culture of America. In view of the part played by German emigrants in moulding the fundamental structure of America and because of the bonds of friendship and blood kinship between the two peoples, it was inevitable that German pedagogs should eventually come to the conclusion that our literary as well as our scientific achievements ought to receive greater attention. The narrow view, stubbornly adhered to for many years, that instruction in English should deal with purely English authors gave place to a determination to include the advancing and progressive American *Volkstum* in the school program.

---

[11] In this category Sintenis places *Tom Sawyer, Huckleberry Finn, Life on the Mississippi, The Innocents Abroad, The Gilded Age,* and *The American Claimant.*

One of the first among German educators to interest himself in Mark Twain as reading for the schools was Dr. Emil Lobedanz,[12] a Gymnasium professor at Schwerin in Mecklenburg. In 1895 he prepared an abridged school edition[13] of *The Prince and the Pauper*.[14] In order to satisfy the requirements of the school library he found it necessary to reduce the original text by more than one half. He met the difficulties of such a drastic condensation by deleting principally detailed descriptions of court ceremony and adventures which had only a very loose connection with the thread of the action, even though they contained some very attractive and effective features. Changes in the language itself were imperative, but these were reduced to a minimum so as not to alter the character of the work or diminish its artistic value. Lobedanz was attracted to this particular work by the charming picture of English customs and traditions at the time of Henry VIII, by the author's remarkable penetration into the feelings and impressions of a "boy's heart," and by the vigorous and soul-stirring language.[15] The text was most favorably received. The reviewers[16] were unanimous in their approval of the fascinating content as a school-text, although they regarded with apprehension the peculiar nature of the "American" language.

Five years later, the Freytag Verlag of Leipsic commissioned Dr. Gustav Krüger,[17] professor at the Kaiser Wilhelms-Realgymnasium in Berlin and one of the most widely known German

---

[12] Lobedanz had previously published *Über das französische Element in Gottfried von Strassburgs Tristan* (1878) and *Der Unterricht in Lektüre und Grammatik, besonders im Französischen* (1890).

[13] This was done for a series of textbooks published by Gärtner of Berlin and known as the "Schulbibliothek französischer und englischer Prosaschriften aus der neueren Zeit."

[14] Berlin: Gärtner, 1895.

[15] *Ibid.*, Introduction, p. 2.

[16] J. Ellinger, *Anglia: Beiblatt*, VI, 45 ff. Ad. Müller, *Archiv für das Studium der neueren Sprachen und Literatur*, XCV, 312 f.

[17] Krüger (1859-1922) joined the faculty of the Kaiser Wilhelms-Realgymnasium in Berlin in 1884. With the exception of a few years when he served as instructor in the War Academy and as "Lektor" in the Technical Institute, Krüger had charge of English literature instruction in the Gymnasium until his retirement in 1916. His scholarly output included a *Systematic English-German Vocabulary* (1893) and an extensive work, *Schwierigkeiten des Englischen:* Vol. I, *Synonymik und Wortgebrauch* (1896); Vol. II, *Syntax* (1898); III, *Vermischte Beiträge zur Syntax* (1904); and Vol. IV, *Unenglisches Englisch* (1911). He also prepared a series of five volumes of English textbooks for the "Schulbücher-Verlag" of Gustav Freytag.

teachers of English, to prepare an abridged school-edition of *The Adventures of Tom Sawyer*.[18] Like Lobedanz, Krüger was compelled to omit many adventures, particularly those which revealed a predilection for "the strange and frightful." These omissions, however, in no wise impaired the interest of the work for German youth. That German boys might discern in Tom Sawyer a reflection of their own inner life made his experiences, in the eyes of some critics[19] at least, most satisfactory school reading. A few[20] of these critics are, to be sure, reluctant to recommend it because of the abundant use of Americanisms and slang. They are by no means convinced that such material lends itself to class instruction. A majority of the commentators, however, was of the opinion that its æsthetic as well as the autobiographical value should assure the book a sympathetic reception into the course of study.[21]

The introduction of *A Tramp Abroad*[22] into the school curriculum in 1903 by Dr. Max Friedrich Mann,[23] a widely-known *Germanist,* is more easily comprehensible from the point of view of content and interest. Mann felt quite assured that the peculiar nature of the subject matter, which dealt with the author's experiences in Germany, would carry not merely a sectional but a general appeal. German critical opinion was, however, divided on its suitability as a school-text. Wilhelm Swoboda,[24] philologist and philosopher, for example, finds the work on the whole commendable, but he takes vigorous exception to the chapter "The Great French Duel," in which Mark Twain satirizes the bloodless French "publicity-duels," for the youthful reader might accept the prodigiously exaggerated caricature as an adequate basis for

[18] Leipsic: Freytag, 1900.

[19] For example, J. Ellinger, *Anglia: Beiblatt*, XII, 148.

[20] Ph. Wagner, *Englische Studien*, XXX, 165. M. Krummacher, *Die Neueren Sprachen*, IX, 546.

[21] Cf. note 19, *supra.*

[22] Leipsic: Freytag, 1903.

[23] For years Dr. Mann was on the editorial staff of *Anglia: Beiblatt, Diesterwegs neusprachliche Reformausgabe,* and *Beiträge zur Geschichte der romanischen Sprachen und Literaturen* (1911). In addition to the Mark Twain edition, Mann also prepared for publication *Lafontaines Fabeln* (1891) and Shakespeare's *Julius Caesar* (1901).

[24] Swoboda was professor at the Landesoberrealschule, Graz, Steiermark, and the author of *John Heywood als Dramatiker* (1888) and *Englische Leselehre* (1889).

judging French conditions. Such a situation, in his opinion, would invalidate one of the foremost objectives of modern language instruction, namely, the just evaluation of "the peculiar foreign spirit."[25] Huendgen, a teacher of Aachen, readily admits that the American judgment of German conditions and customs is interesting and delightful reading for an adult; but he rejects the entire work for German youth on the ground that the instructional value of the material does not justify the student's expenditure of time.[26]

It is interesting to note that in the mind of at least one German educator Mark Twain was associated with Rudyard Kipling. For the school edition of *Five Tales by Rudyard Kipling and Mark Twain*,[27] Dr. Fritz Kriete of Halle a. S. chose two sketches[28] from Mark Twain's *A Tramp Abroad* as representative of the author's style and humor. Though one does not ordinarily place Mark Twain in the same category with Kipling, one might find justification for such a procedure in graphic descriptions and wholesome humor that are common to both.

As for the publications that appeared between 1895 and 1897 inclusive,[29] there is excellent reason to believe that these too were well received. In view of the fact that all these works were considered sufficiently interesting to merit translation within the next year or so, it is rather surprising that only two received consideration in reviews, and that only one of the latter can be said to contain enlightening suggestions. The critical review[30] of *Joan of Arc*

[25] *Die Neueren Sprachen,* XI, 223 f.

[26] *Gymnasium,* XXIII, 49 f.

[27] Halle: Hermann Gesenius, 1903.

[28] "A Restless Night," an account of an experience in Heilbronn, and "A Trip to the Rigi-Kulm."

[29] During these years Tauchnitz continued to publish additional works of Mark Twain as they appeared: one volume of *Pudd'nhead Wilson* in 1895, two volumes of *Personal Recollections of Joan of Arc by the Sieur Louis de Conte, freely translated from the Ancient French into Modern English by Jean Francois Alden* in 1896, two volumes of *More Tramps Abroad* and one volume of *Tom Sawyer, Detective, as told by Huck Finn and other Tales* in 1897. The popularity of the sketches was on the increase, for Mark Twain's *Die Millionpfundnote, Humoreske* was published by two firms: the one with twenty-five illustrations by R. A. Jaumann in a collection of illustrated novels and short stories known as "Kürschners Bücherschatz," the other in stenographic form in the "Büchersammlung für Gabelsberger Stenographie, herausgegeben von Wilhelm Marnet" (1897).

[30] *Archiv für das Studium der neueren Sprachen,* XCIX, 131 ff.

by Dr. Rudolf Fischer,[31] professor of the English language and literature in the University of Innnsbruck and a recognized Shakespeare scholar, commends itself to our consideration primarily for the light it throws on Mark Twain as a novelist. With Shakespeare's dramatic *Historie* as the basis of comparison, Fischer directs attention first of all to a marked resemblance between the drama and the novel. In both, he points out, there is a happy blending of the historical and poetic demands of the material; in both the external truth is subordinated to the inner; and in both the author's individuality breaks through unconsciously in the comprehension and shaping of the cultural ideas of the material. But while Shakespeare thinks as an Elizabethan, Mark Twain approaches the Middle Ages "as a son of our externally rationalistic age with its transcendental instincts." A comparison with Shakespeare's work also affords our critic the opportunity of stressing a fundamental difference in technique. Shakespeare, he says, presents his "Pucelle" in the framework of the drama, with its emphasis upon forceful and vigorous effects, as a "demoniacal witch," and Schiller his Joan as a *Wunderkind*, each according to his principle and point of view. Mark Twain, on the other hand, shows within the framework of the novel an organic development of the character of Joan, which, although retaining the veil of mysticism, is nevertheless convincing and comprehensible in all its objective phases of life. The powerful impression produced by the "profoundly emotional characterization" of Joan is to be attributed to an unsurpassing ability in the discreet employment of the artistic means of the novel.

Just as in 1891, so also again in 1898 Mark Twain's visit to Europe was an important factor in arousing interest in his personality and work.[32] Many of the firms in Austria and Germany wished to capitalize on the current interest in and enthusiasm for Mark Twain which found an admirable expression in the chronic-

[31] Fischer (1860-1923) was widely respected for his *Thomas Middleton, eine literarische Skizze* (1898). His chief distinction was gained from his rather extensive work, *Zu den Kunstformen des mittelalterlichen Epos*, in the "Wiener Beiträge zur englischen Philologie." Shortly after his death, a student of his, Dr. Karl Brunner, edited and published a work on which Fischer had labored for many years, *Shakespeares Sonette* (Gruppierung, Kunstform), 1925.

[32] Paine describes the extraordinary friendly reception among the high and low in Weggis, Switzerland, and Vienna. *Op. cit.*, III, 1043-1076.

ling of his every activity in the daily papers. Although Tauchnitz issued only three volumes[33] within the next seven years (1898-1904), Lutz found it expedient, on the basis of an unusually successful circulation of his six-volume edition of *Ausgewählte humoristische Schriften* of 1892, to put out an illustrated edition of this series in 1898. The text of this edition was identical with that of 1892. It surpassed the earlier edition, however, in the sympathetic and interpretative pictures which were contributed by two very gifted artists.[34] This added feature unquestionably contributed much to the strong appeal of this edition. Lutz followed with a "railroad edition"[35] of the same series in 1899 and 1900, a new edition of six volumes of *Mark Twains ausgewählte humoristische Schriften. Neue Folge*[36] in 1902, and in 1904 a juvenile edition of *Tom Sawyers Abenteuer und Streiche* and *Huck Finns Fahrten und Abenteuer* in a series known as "Mark Twains humoristische Schriften für die Jugend." These, supplemented by the publications of the constantly rising number of firms[37] which seemed to take at least a straggling interest in

[33] Two volumes of *The Man That Corrupted Hadleyburg, and Other Stories and Sketches* in 1900; one volume of *A Double-barreled Detective Story* in 1902.

[34] Albert Richter and H. Schrödter.

[35] This edition was also identical in content with those of 1892 and 1898.

[36] Vol. I, *Tom Sawyers neue Abenteuer (Tom Sawyer im Luftballon. Tom, der kleine Detektiv)*—the latter appeared separately for the first time in 1901; Vol. II, *Querkopf Wilson*, which had already appeared in Lutz' "Sammlung ausgewählter Kriminal- und Detektiv-Romane" with a second and third edition in 1901; Vols. III and IV, *Meine Reise um die Welt*, a German version of *More Tramps Abroad* which Lutz had issued as early as 1898 in a rather expensive binding; Vol. V, *Adams Tagebuch und andere Erzählungen*, with a first printing in 1901; and Vol. VI, *Wie Hadleyburg verderbt wurde*, which Lutz had published in 1900.

[37] In 1898 R. Jacobsthal, a Berlin publisher, attempted to compete with Lutz in a series of translations of detective stories known as "Amerikanische Detektiv-romane." In order to give his series "a touch of real literary flavor," Jacobsthal added a volume by Mark Twain and Edgar Allen Poe entitled *Der junge Detektiv und andere Kriminalgeschichten*. Reclam issued the sixth and last volume of his *Ausgewählte Skizzen*. In addition to the special Lutz edition of *Tom Sawyers Abenteuer* in 1900, Hillger of Berlin published a translation by Thomas Bürk with illustrations by W. Roegge in his "Kürschners Bücherschatz." Hendel of Halle also added a translation by H. Hellwag for his "Bibliothek der Gesamtliteratur des In- und Auslandes." *The Prince and the Pauper* appeared in German form in a collection published by A. Pichler Witwe & Sohn of Vienna and known as "Bücherei für die Jugend." This work was translated by Helene Stökl, who was already well known as a short story writer and novelist. In 1902 Hendel also published a translation of *Huckleberry Finn* by Hellwag in his "Bibliothek der Gesamtliteratur des In- und Auslandes" as *Die Abenteuer Huckleberry Finns*. In 1901 Meyers Volksbücher

Mark Twain, must be credited with consolidating the ever-increasing popularity of the American humorist in Germany.

Much of the success of the *Illustrated Edition* of Mark Twain's works which Lutz published in 1898 must be attributed to the extreme care with which it was prepared. The elaborate format was held to match, in every respect, the excellence of the translation. In some quarters the opinion was expressed that no native author within recollection had ever received such generous consideration from a publisher. There was, however, one feature of this edition which aroused pointed dissatisfaction. In a critical evaluation of Mark Twain's work in the *Gegenwart*,[38] an influential weekly devoted to politics, literature, and art, Carl von Thaler,[39] an Austrian author and journalist associated with the *Neue Freie Presse* of Vienna, takes vigorous exception to the practice of prefacing an edition of this kind with a literary appraisal of the author, declaring that such an appreciation is rarely authoritative and that it frequently tends to antagonize the reader. In the present case he is especially irked by the frequently expressed yet wholly unwarranted verdict that Mark Twain is "the greatest humorist in the world." He rejects, without reservation, every attempt to compare Mark Twain with the author of *Pickwick Papers* and *Master Humphrey's Clock,* either in drastic comedy of situation or in depth of feeling. Even Bret Harte he esteems superior, while Frank Stockton and other American humorists are judged Mark Twain's equals. Among the Viennese and Berlin contemporaries he finds many who can readily compete with him. Nevertheless, von Thaler does not underestimate the value of Mark Twain's work. His resentment is directed primarily against the German "deification" of Mark Twain.

Von Thaler entitles his article "Mark Twain in Deutschland," and we are probably justified in regarding his appraisal as a synthesis of the attitude of a large section of public opinion. When

---

brought out an additional translation of some of Mark Twain's stories by H. Löwe under the title *Erzählungen und Plaudereien.*

[38] LX (1899), 376 ff.

[39] Although a student of classical and oriental philology, Carl von Thaler gained his chief distinction as an exceptionally well qualified political journalist. Over a considerable period of years he contributed many editorials and feuilletons with a pronounced German national feeling.

he characterizes the *Sketches* as "Mark Twain's strong side," or as "a literary snapshot," or as "an ornament of American literature," he undoubtedly formulates the well-nigh unanimous view of informed circles. The importance which he attaches to the aphorisms as a source of "spiritual nature and the conduct of life" also attracted considerable critical support. But it is questionable whether there was the same inclination on the part of German critics at this time to value so highly the descriptions of travel contained in *The Innocents Abroad* and *More Tramps Abroad*. Although there is much that von Thaler rejects, he nevertheless finds these descriptions particularly revealing for the omissions which, by implication, may explain Mark Twain's character as well as his art.

A point of more than minor interest to our study is von Thaler's attitude toward *The Adventures of Tom Sawyer* and *The Adventures of Huckleberry Finn*. The natural disposition on the part of some German commentators to classify them as novels is strongly challenged on the ground that the element of love, indispensable to a novel, is utterly lacking. Since the relations between the sexes offer to the humorist opportunity for some of the most ridiculous as well as the most sublime transformations of reality, he finds it strange that with the sole exception of the *Millionenbanknote* Mark Twain disregarded the most powerful of human passions. Although he takes note of this interesting fact, von Thaler makes no attempt to explain it. Incidentally he feels that German youth should benefit greatly by the convincing, effective, and unusually vivid presentation of mischievous pranks and adventures which, to his mind, are possible only in America or perhaps in the imagination of an American.

There is no doubt that towards the turn of the century the name of Mark Twain had imprinted itself deeply on the imagination of the German-speaking people. His own personal appearances in Germany, Austria, and Switzerland, recorded in abundant references and notices in the public press, were, as we have seen, contributory factors. What impression the rank and file of German readers had of our American humorist is problematical. Though everyone heard and spoke of Mark Twain, it is more than probable that there were relatively few who based their conception of him on a study of his works. A public character such as Mark Twain, particularly if he happens to be a humorist by profession, naturally calls forth many and diverse comments. These impressions are repeated, and, combined with individual reactions, produce more or less false ideas of his personality.

There is, indeed, convincing evidence that erroneous conceptions of Mark Twain were becoming prevalent among German readers. These were now reaching such unprecedented numbers that a highly respected Catholic interpreter, well able to deal constructively with Mark Twain, found it advisable to come to the defense of the American humorist. In his study, "Mark Twain als Mensch und Humorist,"[40] which is revealing in its analysis of Mark Twain's moral and psychological development, A. Wurm turns first of all to a refutation of the most commonly held view, namely, that Mark Twain is a mere entertainer or buffoon, whose life purpose it is to amuse Europe as well as America. Rejecting this interpretation as having no basis in fact, Wurm sets forth in sharp contrast the thesis that Mark Twain is rather an absolutely independent personality with no desire to court the approval of the masses. In support of this he analyzes the tremendous formative influence of his rigorous training and experience as a pilot on the Mississippi. Three very decisive results are particularly stressed: the subjugation of any desire for honor by the public and a corresponding ennoblement of an inborn passion for greatness in itself; a firm control over a certain cowardice and an impetuous temperament; and, equally significant, the subordination of feeling to energy of the will and keenness of mind. In this connection he recalls the frequently voiced charge, in which he concurs, that Mark Twain lacks depth of feeling. To clarify his position, Wurm draws an interesting contrast between Mark Twain and Nietzsche. Comparing the former with a cold, rugged mountain and the latter with a volcano, he reaches the conclusion that Mark Twain would never have developed such independence of spirit and such perfect ethical equilibrium if he had possessed the volcanic fire or emotional power of a Nietzsche; for Nietzsche was not master of

---

[40] *Alte und neue Welt,* XXXVIII (1903-1904), 718-720.

himself even though he emphasized the principle of unconditional power for the superman. He was rather a victim of his own intensity of feeling.

Wurm then proceeds to a refutation of another misconception, the assertion of certain commentators that a humorist has no *Weltanschauung*. Starting with the assumption that Mark Twain is a wholesome ethical personality and that a *Weltanschauung* forms the very essence of such a personality, our critic seeks to prove on the basis of his record in *Life on the Mississippi* that Mark Twain has a *Weltanschauung*, which in its essential features is to be derived from the established characteristics of his personality. Defining *Weltanschauung* as "the most profound, powerful, and all-controlling mainspring of human thought, feeling, and action," Wurm points out that it would be inaccurate to characterize Mark Twain's *Weltanschauung* as Christian, inasmuch as Christian influences played no part in the development of his personality. For want of a better term he calls it "modern," because in accordance with the author's vigorous character, it places emphasis predominantly upon cultural progress. But this progress is conditioned by the loyalty and respect of a nation for its laws, which are the security of a prosperous and salutary development. The progress of civilization expressed in terms of physical achievements forms accordingly the highest norm by which mankind is measured. The fact that Mark Twain emphasizes the influence of law as the guiding principle of a heterogeneous people, our critic attributes directly to the tremendous influence of personal experience and life itself upon his individual development.

Although Wurm concedes that Mark Twain may thus approach a Christian *Weltanschauung*, he nevertheless takes the position, which he supports with documentary references, that the American humorist is in reality fundamentally foreign to it. Mark Twain's *Weltanschauung*, he says, places sharp emphasis upon an energetic activity of the spirit, expressed in terms of the human will and human power, as the fundamental basis of a nation's true prosperity. Since this spirit of activity is not grounded in Christianity but is rather a product of human autonomy, it deprives

Christianity of every essential influence upon the welfare and mis-
fortunes, happiness and sorrows of a nation, and of every positive,
standardizing, and regulatory influence on human life. Thus it
illustrates the old titanic, heathen spirit which Christianity sought
strenuously to conquer in Pelagianism. Wurm, however, does not
believe that Mark Twain is conscious of this antithesis to Christianity. He finds ample ground for his deduction in the fact that
Mark Twain's work discloses a heart receptive for that which is
noble, altruistic, and liberal.

Closely linked to the ethical development of Mark Twain's
personality is also its æsthetic growth in the direction of humor.[41]
Following a procedure initiated by former German critics, Wurm
employs German humor as the standard of measurement in order
to determine the character of American humor as represented by
Mark Twain. As an illustration he instances a humorous passage
from Peter Rosegger's *Als ich noch der Waldbauernbub war.*[42]
American humor, he finds, lacks the "profound inner world" of
the German. Mark Twain did at times make honest endeavors to
strike this chord, but those very efforts do not carry conviction.
Mark Twain's humor moves rather in the "sphere of the intellect"; its effect does not penetrate into the depths of human feeling. Consequently the object of his humor does not arouse sympathy, but an objective mental satisfaction which expresses itself
eventually in laughter. German humor, on the other hand, causes
the reader to submerge a part of his ego into that of the hero,
while the other part hovers supreme over the entire situation,
thereby achieving an objective, mental satisfaction, and also calling into activity "a most profound phase of the soul." Judged by
German standards, critics might argue that Mark Twain's humor
is not humor at all; Wurm, however, takes the view that even
though the sphere of German humor is quite different from that of
the American, Mark Twain's humor is nevertheless humor, but a
humor that depends for its effect upon the most subtle psychologi-

[41] *Ibid.*, pp. 748-751.
[42] Wurm selects the story of Talertoni and the accompanying "rosary scene" as
illustrating the essence of German humor. In content it is very closely analogous to
the selection from *Life on the Mississippi* which describes the harassed conscience
of a boy who believed he was guilty of causing a drunkard's death.

cal motivation. The truer and the more natural this motivation, the sharper, the more clearly outlined, and the more vigorous is the pleasure awakened in the soul of the reader, who realizes that all emotions have been grossly exaggerated. In the presentation of this "psychological humor," Wurm contends, Mark Twain is unquestionably a master.

With the approach of Mark Twain's seventieth birthday, it is hardly an exaggeration to say that he was enjoying a popularity in Germany that had attained a height unprecedented in the history of the literary invasion from this side of the ocean. The numerous publications in the years just discussed confirm the impression formed in the early period that German publishers did all in their power to create and to perpetuate a sustained interest in an author who was conspicuously successful in his own country. In this effort they were aided by the atmosphere of mutual goodwill engendered by the author's visits. Generally speaking, the *Sketches* continued to be the most popular of Mark Twain's writings; but there can be no doubt that the two juvenile books, *The Adventures of Tom Sawyer* and *The Adventures of Huckleberry Finn*, increased steadily in popularity, even though the general public esteem is not correspondingly reflected in the rather sparing critical opinion. German criticism, to be sure, does not ignore them, but its comment clearly indicates a cautious and conservative approach. Indeed, the consistently sustained interest of a Tauchnitz or a Lutz is not reflected in the critical material on Mark Twain of these years. To be sure, a large number of journals and periodicals published reviews at various intervals; but, on the whole, they refrained from any extended discussion of Mark Twain and exhibited at most merely a transitory interest and a superficial knowledge.

Various reasons may be assigned for this attitude. In the first place, there were doubtless many critics who, although they admitted that America had assumed leadership in many technical and industrial fields, nevertheless believed that this country had nothing to offer Europe in those of art and science. In the second place, there may have been critics who did not consider humor a legitimate phase of literature and consequently undertook no analysis of Mark Twain's work. Furthermore, there were others who, with German humor as a criterion, were simply unable to understand Mark Twain's American humor. One may indeed apply the characterization of "oft-mentioned but little-known author" not only to the public but to the critics as well.

Notwithstanding the generally repetitious character of the comments on Mark Twain's art, we may note three directions among the critics of these years. There are those who in ardent admiration incline to overemphasize and overestimate his humor; those who attribute cultural and artistic value to his works, an attitude that finds concrete expression in these years in the introduction of Mark Twain into the schools; and those who subscribe to an amusement value, but minimize or deny the cultural and spiritual aspects of his work.

As in the former period, considerable attention is devoted to a discussion of the specifically American character of Mark Twain's humor. It is variously termed "humor of the revolver,"[43] "fantastic humor,"[44] "an unique growth,"[45] "a fantastic, expansive, eccentric humor,"[46] and "a psychological humor."[47] It is made emphatically plain that it is a humor that does not penetrate into the depths of the "soul-world" as does German humor, but exists only in the sphere of "intellect and fancy." When one has correctly understood Mark Twain the man, one knows immediately with absolute certainty that Mark Twain the humorist will reveal "intellect, power, sharp observation, definiteness, clearness of fancy," but not the deep soul of German humor.

There is a decided attempt on the part of critics to refute and correct erroneous conceptions concerning the American author. Critical comments are frequently prefaced with short sketches of his public and personal life, and these lay particular stress on those experiences which characterize him as man and humorist. For it is generally agreed that an intelligent comprehension of Mark Twain the humorist is contingent upon a knowledge and understanding of

---

[43] von Thaler, *Die Gegenwart*, LV (1899), 377.
[44] *Beilage zur Allgemeinen Zeitung*, May 6, 1896, p. 5.
[45] Introduction to *Tom Sawyers Streiche und Abenteuer* (Stuttgart: Lutz, 1892).
[46] Dr. Karl Ludwig Schleich, *Die Zukunft*, November 19, 1898, p. 392.
[47] *Alte und neue Welt*, XXXVIII, 750.

Mark Twain the man. Ethically he is recognized as a worthy figure, representing the best the world can fashion without the direct influence of Christianity.

Amid all the complexity and diversity of the critical reaction in this period there is one impression which seems to be in the ascendant. It is best expressed in the words of an anonymous critic in 1899: "Mark Twain is recognized by many—perhaps by those who judge him without knowing him—as a great buffoon, but whoever examines his works will soon find that the American humorist instructs and educates as well as amuses and cheers. No one can read Mark Twain without deriving from his works a lasting, morally invigorating influence."[48]

[48] *Monatsblätter für deutsche Literatur*, III (1898-1899), 34.

III

SEVENTIETH BIRTHDAY AND DEATH
1905-1910

On the thirtieth of November, 1905, Mark Twain celebrated his seventieth birthday. Not only America but the entire world took cognizance of this and paid tribute to his unusual character and attainments. The press in Germany and Austria took advantage of this opportunity to express its gratitude and appreciation. Almost without exception the prominent newspapers of these countries carried articles by distinguished literary journalists of the day. A similar situation recurred at the time of Mark Twain's death on the twenty-first of April, 1910. Again the press of Germany and Austria and the German language press of Hungary paid tribute to the memory of so rare and rich a personality. Newspapers and journals which had not hitherto concerned themselves with Mark Twain published articles by writers familiar with American literature. The fact that the authors of these monographs approach Mark Twain in very much the same spirit as the anniversary commentators of 1905 makes it advisable, in spite of the five-year interval, to review their observations as one contribution.

Before proceeding to examine this body of critical opinion, however, we should survey the activity of the publishers during this period. The extent of their effort to sustain and extend his popularity will enable us to measure his vogue among German readers.

The year 1905 brought merely supplementary editions of the *Sketches* and *The Prince and the Pauper*. Hesse of Leipsic issued two slender volumes[1] of sketches in German, and O. Spamer[2] of

---

[1] These appeared as volumes 226 and 237 in a series known as "Hesses Volksbücherei": the one, a booklet of some ninety-four pages, selling for the modest sum of twenty pfennigs, entitled *Die 1,000,000 Pfundnote und andere humoristische Erzählungen und Skizzen* (the translations were furnished by M. Jacobi, H. Koch, and L. Ottman), and the other, *Tot oder Lebendig. Erzählungen und Skizzen.*

[2] The edition which O. Spamer issued as *Prinz und Bettler* was a translation by Professor Rudolf Brunner, an East-Prussian schoolmaster. Brunner considered it Mark Twain's most charming work, and presented it to German youth for the

Leipsic and Loewes[3] of Stuttgart a volume each containing *The Prince and the Pauper*. In addition to a *Wörterbuch*[4] of some forty-six pages, the following year brought only an edition of Mark Twain's *Wie Tom den Zaum anstrich*.[5] Two years later A. Weichert of Berlin published a volume of *Die Abenteuer Tom Sawyers* and a volume of *Die Abenteuer Huckleberry Finns, des Kameraden von Tom Sawyer*.[6] That *Tom Sawyer* was increasing in popularity is evidenced by the fact that in 1910 Fr. Schulze published a stenographic version in German of some 96 pages of selections from the book.[7] After a lapse of five years, Tauchnitz issued in 1907 a volume in English containing *Christian Science. With Notes concerning Corrections to Date* and a volume of *The $30,000 Bequest and other Stories*, consisting of some twenty-seven narratives and sketches of varying length and unequal literary value.[8] Although *Captain Stormfield's Visit to Heaven* and *Is Shakespeare Dead?* had appeared in book form in the United States in 1907 and 1909 respectively, they did not appear in the Tauchnitz Library until 1910. Of these new volumes, two attracted the attention of the German critics.

In July of 1909, A. Rambeau of Berlin-Wilmersdorf, an associate editor of *Die Neueren Sprachen*, published in that journal an essay, *Mark Twain on Christain Science*, by M. Fischer of Berkeley, California. Fischer presents, not a critical estimate of the work, but merely an objective discussion of Mark Twain's

---

great moral value inherent in the spirit of Christian fellowship which it contains. The text was accompanied by illustrations by G. A. Stroedel. The work was sufficiently well received to necessitate a second printing in 1908 and a third issue in 1911.

[3] Helene Lobedan, who, as early as 1890, had made a translation of *The Prince and the Pauper* for Ricker of Giessen, supplied the German translation for Loewes, who published it as *Prinz und Bettelknabe. Eine Erzählung für die reifere Jugend*. The attractiveness of this edition was enhanced considerably by the thirty-six illustrations by Willy Planck.

[4] For the school edition of *A Tramp Abroad*, which appeared in 1901.

[5] Vol. XLVII of "Lutz Kriminal- und Detektiv-Romane."

[6] Each volume contained an introduction by Albert Erding (literary pseudonym of Walter Heichen of Berlin-Steglitz), who is known for his translations of Dickens, Byron, Scott, Poe, Wallace's *Ben Hur*, and a few *Kriminalromane* of modern writers.

[7] This appeared in the series "Sammlung berühmter ausländischer Schriftsteller. In vereinfachter deutscher Stenographie, System Stolze-Schrey," (Serie I: IX).

[8] Teichmann, *Neue philologische Rundschau*, XXV, 593 f. (December 14, 1907).

attitude toward Christian Science. He examines particularly his satirical condemnation of the movement and the amusing exposé of the business conduct and guiding character behind it. This article was published in English and introduced by a preface on Christian Science in German by Rambeau, which is not without interest as a German evaluation of American character.

The other work, *Is Shakespeare Dead?*, precipitated a lively controversy among German philologians. It is of more than casual interest, inasmuch as it again brought into the limelight the discussion of the "Shakespeare tradition," the relation or identity between the author Shakespeare and the actor Shaxper. The reaction of the German critics towards this work reflects again their radically diverse attitudes towards Mark Twain as a whole. There are those who see in him primarily the humorist and accordingly interpret his *Is Shakespeare Dead?* as the work of a wag, far removed from naïveté, sentimentality, satire, or philosophy. On the other hand, there are others who are disinclined to think of Mark Twain merely as a humorist and who accept the work as the most important product of his genius. These contrasting attitudes are best set forth by Rudolf Fischer, a recognized Shakespeare scholar of the University of Innsbruck, in his discussion in the *Jahrbuch der deutschen Shakespeare-Gesellschaft*,[9] and by Gustav Holzer,[10] a professor at the Oberrealschule in Heidelberg, in the *Heidelberger Tageblatt*.[11]

In order properly to evaluate the significance of Mark Twain's *Is Shakespeare Dead?*, Professor Fischer gives a brief but suggestive introductory analysis of Goethe's *Faust* in so far as it concerns the latter's magic power of appeal. Classifying readers

[9] XLVI (1910), 258 f.

[10] Professor Holzer was particularly interested in the Shakespeare problem. In 1908 he published a study of some thirty-three pages entitled *Shakespeare im Lichte der neuesten Forschung*, in which he supported the English-American view of Lord Bacon's authorship. The following year brought an essay, *Kuno Fischers irrige Erklärungen der Poetik Bacons*, and *Ein Kommentar zu Shakespeares Drama Julius Caesar*. In 1910 and 1911 the battle cry "Hier Shakespeare-hier Bacon-Shakespeare" was often heard. In 1910 Sir Edwin Durning-Lawrence published *Bacon Is Shakespeare*, together with a reprint of Bacon's *Promus of Formalities and Elegancies*. This book was extensively reviewed in German circles. On the basis of this work, Holzer wrote his article, *Das Shakespeare-Problem*.

[11] June 26, 1909.

as naïve, sentimental, satirical, and philosophical, he shows how that work captures the imagination of the individual groups. The naïve reader, he points out, is impressed by a popular, simple story; the sentimental reader by the vital needs of the poet in the portrayal of his searching hero; the satiric reader by Mephisto's universal skepticism; and the philosophically inclined by "the profound fate of mankind." But, in the opinion of our critic, the highly variant impressions which the reader receives, according to his power of reception, should be attributed, not to the individual elements—situations or figures—which alternately hold the attention, but to the whole, the totality, which works simultaneously in diverse ways. *Faust* as well as Shakespeare's dramas, Fischer contends, owes its imperishability primarily to the fact that it appeals to all classes of people. Viewed in this light, he comes to the conclusion that Mark Twain's *Is Shakespeare Dead?* should be ranked as one of those rare epic works of art that are, through their very nature, of manifold appeal. The naïve reader unfamiliar with the facts of Shakespeare's biography and the cultural phenomena of the Elizabethan era, and equally unenlightened as to the distinction between scholarly work and artistic production, is convinced by the reasoning: since we know nothing about Shakespeare, since his contemporaries knew very little about him, since their successors knew nothing about him, therefore Shakespeare was himself ignorant, especially about the intricacies of jurisprudence. His conclusion is that, since the dramas presuppose so much education and legal training, Shakespeare could not have written them. The sentimental reader, Fischer points out, is more drawn to the author than to the book itself. He is pleased that Mark Twain, now seventy and famous, is pursued by the fiery zeal of an idealistic youth in his twenties to tear the mask from the face of a forger and to assist Bacon in his claim to authorship against Shakespeare. The satirical reader, Mephisto himself, smiles in a friendly, cunning way as he glances into the cards of the roguish author. He realizes that the author intermingles tradition and twaddle in order to excoriate Shakespeare and that he exchanges with a conjurer's rapidity poetry and scholarship so as to take sides with Bacon. The philosophically inclined reader, our critic asserts, will interpret the work symbolically. He will recognize the ambitious attempt to discredit and destroy a great author, Shakespeare, by comparing him with another great man, Bacon, who assumes thereby still greater stature. Fischer, however, does not believe that the work would appeal to the naïve reader. This consideration prompts him to ask whether Mark Twain is not just what he always was when one reads him "naturally"—merely the rogue, nothing more than the simple, and therefore great, humorist. In his opinion, which many well-informed Americans share, Mark Twain writes on behalf of Bacon as the author of Shakespeare's works in order to perpetrate a capital hoax, thereby destroying a literary-historical scandal in his own inimitable way.

Gustav Holzer, on the other hand, sets himself sharply against such an interpretation. In his opinion, Mark Twain's work is not "a tremendous joke or hoax" nor a "godless book of a childish old man," but rather the most important work from the author's pen. Personally convinced of the sincerity and earnestness of the old "Nestor of fictional writings," Holzer endorses Mark Twain's argument that the author Shake-speare and Francis Bacon were one and the same person and that the dramas were written, not by the actor Shaxper, but by the author Shakespeare (Bacon), who was unquestionably a highly educated and a thoroughly competent jurist.[12] The embarrassment in the Shaxper camp, as reflected in the opinions of Mark Twain's opponents in various American and English newspapers, provides, in our critic's opinion, additional evidence of the credibility and soundness of that view. Even a superficial analysis of the critical comments, he contends, reveals no material to refute the "author-Shakespeare" argument, or to substantiate further the claim of the "idol Shaxper or Shakspere." Nor is he able to find in these defendants of the tradition any explanation for the difference in writing the names "Shake-speare" and "Shakspere." The disparaging criticism of Mark Twain's work, in Holzer's opinion, may be attributed to the disinclination of some readers to be aroused from

[12] Holzer calls attention to the fact that Mark Twain is indebted to G. G. Greenwood for his principal argument in behalf of Bacon. Cf. G. G. Greenwood, M.P., *The Shakespeare Case Re-stated*. London: John Lane, 1908.

their lethargy and in others to the tendency to reject every attempt at an innovation or an approach to a sensible rational solution as "an indiscreet piece of arrogance or an unjustifiable disturbance."

It would be an error to assume that the two works, *Christian Science* and *Is Shakespeare Dead?*, played more than a minor rôle in the formation of German opinion regarding Mark Twain. Neither of them was translated; they appeared only in the Tauchnitz Library and consequently reached only a limited number of German readers. But in spite of their inaccessibility to the German public at large, they are of interest to our study in so far as they indicate an extension of the knowledge of our American author in educated circles. For an evaluation of Mark Twain's position among the masses in these years we must turn to the anniversary tributes of 1905 and to the necrologies of 1910.

In general, it may be said that these writings recall with considerable interest and obvious satisfaction the originality and variety of his life, the colorful significance of his pen name, and his remarkably curious succession of unforgettable experiences and achievements. "Personality" stories, anecdotes which illustrate the qualities of his humor, aphorisms which reveal the "smiling philosopher,"[13] and extracts from his works are brought forward in an effort to stress those traits which, taken collectively, tend to give a composite picture of our American humorist. Though such observations had found expression here and there in former years, emphasis on them at a time when the entire world was paying homage to him as one of the outstanding literary personalities of recent times throws a dramatic light on the powerful appeal of his personality. His unprecedented popularity is acknowledged[14] and a number of explanations are advanced for his wide-spread vogue.

[13] *Hamburger Correspondent*, No. 30, 1905.

[14] Fritz Baumann (*National-Zeitung*, Berlin, November 30, 1905), for example, characterizes Mark Twain as "one of the foremost in the ranks of American authors in the field of humor"; Eduard Pötzl (*Neues Wiener Tagblatt*, November 30, 1905) as "one who has the *Lacher* of the entire world on his side"; Benno Diederich (*Tägliche Rundschau*, November 30, 1905) as "the best known and the most significant humorist among foreign authors who are just as well known to the German reader as certain outstanding personalities of native literature"; and Rudolf Fürst (*Vossische Zeitung*, November, 1905) as "the most powerful among the few humorous talents, one of the wittiest men of the century," a genius, even though perhaps

One of the most plausible of these conjectures was made by Eduard Pötzl in the *Neues Wiener Tagblatt*.[15] Pötzl began his career as a reporter in the circuit courts of Vienna, where he had ample opportunity to observe and study the psychology of his own people. His sympathetic understanding and humorous interpretations of their problems, evidenced by his criminal *humoresques* and descriptions of the proletariat, received early recognition and led to an appointment on the editorial staff of the *Neues Wiener Tagblatt*. From that day until his death in 1914 he enjoyed the reputation of being one of the foremost humorists and feuilletonists of Vienna. In view of the circumstance that he was also intimately acquainted with Mark Twain, he may be regarded as the best qualified of all the commentators to analyze the various factors in the public reaction. Mark Twain's popularity he attributes, first of all, to the anecdotes which persistently found their way into the daily papers.[16] The fact that hundreds ot thousands of people in all lands who have never read a book of Mark Twain's are as familiar with his name as with those of the greatest of historical personalities, is, in Pötzl's judgment, an obvious result of the constant association of Mark Twain's name with anecdotes. Although he is inclined to share the current impression that the humorist intentionally inspired this persistent advertisement,[17] Pötzl nevertheless finds it difficult to reconcile himself to the assumption that the famous American, like many German authors who find no means too absurd to focus attention on themselves, actually directs it. Personal endeavor, he contends, is unnecessary, for Mark Twain can rely upon a large and intimate circle of friends and followers to spread his jokes.

Among the critics of this period there seems almost unanimous agreement that no other literary man of the day made such extensive use of advertisement or played the rôle of a humorist in life

---

only a fragmentary genius. Leon Kellner (*Neue Freie Presse*, December 3, 1905, p. 32) even contends forcefully that the works of no English or American writer of his day had found so many translations and publications in Germany as Mark Twain's.

[15] November 30, 1905. Nr. 331.

[16] Fritz Baumann (*National-Zeitung*, November 30, 1905) expresses a similar view.

[17] Eduard Lipton, *Wiener Deutsches Tagblatt,* November 30, 1905.

with such publicistic success as Mark Twain. O. von Gottberg,[18] novelist, feuilletonist, and special correspondent for the *Berliner Lokal Anzeiger,* in particular emphasizes the American humorist's skill in arousing public interest in his own person. Mark Twain, he declares, was a humorist, and his conduct had to awaken laughter. He recalls how Mark Twain altered and distorted his daily round, just as he did the action in his narratives, how he changed the normal routine of existence until his own life appeared as grotesque as that of his heroes, and how until his seventieth birthday not a week passed in which he did not express in print his views on events of the day.[19]

The intriguing impression of his personality, which acted as a living continuation of his humorous works, is, in fact, advanced as a peculiarly potent factor of Mark Twain's wide popularity.[20] The public, it is held, found his personal appearance decidedly unusual, particularly in his later years. People were stimulated by his immediate presence, and on innumerable occasions were stirred to admiration by his picturesque attire, inexhaustible wit, and virile bearing.

In other quarters of German opinion Mark Twain's unusual success is attributed to the glorious unconstraint and wholesomeness of the era in which he lived. It was a period, these writers point out, in which a nation was engaged in a tremendous exploitation of its natural resources; a period in which the individual enjoyed an unlimited freedom of development, of public expression, and participation in public assemblage; a period when the atmosphere was saturated with humor and when the national temper insisted on concentrating all "lust for sensation" in a few names and stamping these at any cost as objects of veneration.[21] Moreover, it was an era in which the lecture platform was a well established institution. B. Schidlof, for example, in his comments on Mark Twain in *Aus fremden Zungen,*[22] attaches the utmost im-

---

[18] Gottberg gained considerable recognition as the author of the biography *Theodore Roosevelt,* which was published in 1908.

[19] *Velhagen & Klasings Monatshefte,* June, 1910, p. 273.

[20] Hugo Eick, poet and an interested interpreter of German, French, and English literature, strongly advances this view. *März,* May, 1910, p. 317.

[21] *Ibid.*

[22] XX (1910), 524.

portance to the lecture platform of that time as a means of building up the popularity of an author. It enabled the humorist on lecture tours to speak to hundreds of thousands in various parts of the world, and a large part of these audiences, Schidlof assumes, also purchased his books.

Another favorable factor which is variously considered and stressed by the German commentators in their appraisal of Mark Twain's extensive popularity is the strongly human appeal of his colorful career. Adolf Saager,[23] Swiss author and journalist, in particular points out that German interest in Mark Twain was greatly stimulated by the sharp contrast between the American author's fantastic career, which brought him successively into the public eye as a pilot, soldier, journalist, traveler, lecturer, and man of letters, and the traditional German attitude, which on the one hand, was inclined to question and condemn repeated changes of occupation and on the other, to impute a certain *moralisches Plus* to a constant and honorable attachment to the native soil.[24] The record of Mark Twain's seventy years of adventure in the Old and the New World, through the heights and depths of human life, served to direct the attention of the German reader to a life such as he had found only in the biography of a Cellini or a Cervantes and what is still more significant, to a life that reflected the spirit of an America in which the chief consideration is immediate results and success, not ultimate consequences.

Finally, Mark Twain's popularity at home and abroad, it is contended, owes much to the heroic honesty and iron diligence of Samuel Clemens the business man.[25] In this connection attention is called to the fact that he did not interpret humorously the financial obligations which accrued from his tragic experiences as a publisher, but that he insisted on assuming full responsibility for the debts of his partner. Not only did he become a favorite of his own nation, but multitudes of people in all lands were attracted

[23] Saager was active as a translator and as an author of dramas and political biographical pamphlets. His interest in America led to his translation in 1910 of *Helen Keller-Briefe meiner Kinderzeit*. Later he published *Henry Fords Werden und Wirken* (1924).

[24] *Hamburger Nachrichten*, November 29, 1905.

[25] Gottberg, *Velhagen & Klasings Monatshefte*, June, 1910, p. 272.

by his unique behavior, and took him to their hearts. German opinion, it may be said, leans to the view that the Yankee esteems most highly Samuel Clemens as the unblemished and honest business man whom misfortune could not bend or break but only incite to further activity; that it is not so much Mark Twain the author of whom the Yankee speaks with such evident pride, but Clemens the man of business. For in the latter the nation saw a reflection of its national type. It was this feeling, according to our German critics, that perhaps unconsciously influenced people to buy and to read his books. It was the spontaneous sympathy which frequently appears in cold, calculating, matter-of-fact American business life that attracted the Yankee to purchase Mark Twain's books and to attend his lectures.

Although the critics dwell on what one acute commentator called "the incalculable element in the situation,"[26] it is nevertheless the consensus of well-informed German opinion that Mark Twain's popularity as a whole was the result primarily of his own individual capacities, in the first place, as an instructor and spiritual benefactor of his countrymen, and in the second place, as a humorist.

Although it is conceded that the average German reader knows Mark Twain only through translations, and therefore must necessarily have an incomplete picture of his creative power and of the effect which his writings exerted on his countrymen,[27] nevertheless the more reflective minds among the German critics stress the importance of the cultural value of his work. They see in the development of the author himself a sharp and faithful reflection of the irregular and rapid growth of the American nation. The vivid, kaleidoscopic pictures which he draws of American life in all its complexities are, in their judgment, evidence of his effort to advance his fellowmen. In discussing this phase of Mark Twain's activity, Eduard Lipton of the *Wiener Deutsches Tagblatt*,[28] draws a striking comparison with Benjamin Franklin. Both, he recalls, began as typesetters; both were as much interested in the practical advancement of their countrymen as in their entertain-

[26] Hugo Eick, *März*, May, 1910, p. 317.
[27] *Ibid.*, November 30, 1905. Nr. 331.
[28] *Idem.*

ment and spiritual elevation; both were politicians as well as philosophers; both showed the practical American spirit which seeks the useful in everything. Franklin gave the world the lightning rod; although the practical inventions of the author Mark Twain are not so important, his inventions dealing with insignificant practical improvements nevertheless give evidence of the same spirit.

The observation that Mark Twain's chief title to fame rests upon the wide appeal of his humor finds also considerable critical support in the tributes of 1905 and 1910. This comes to light in the inevitable comparisons that are drawn between the German and the American humorists, on the one hand, and between Mark Twain and his American contemporaries on the other. Pötzl, for example, contends that no German humorist, with the possible exception of Wilhelm Busch, can ever compete successfully with a humorist writing in the English language. Deriving his effectiveness from his native soil, the German is too much preoccupied with the local and sentimental, with the result that his works are frequently not understood, even in a neighboring province. The fact that Fritz Reuter, the Low-German author, has just recently been translated into the High German; that the Palatine writer Barack is practically unknown outside of the Rheinland; that Wilhelm Raabe, the North German, is not justly appreciated in South Germany and Austria; and that no German humorist has ever been translated into English, must be attributed, he maintains, primarily to the parochial nature of German humor. This factor is also advanced as an explanation for the inability of many humorous authors of less importance, such as the Americans Stockton and Aldrich, to gain an interested reading public in Germany. Their humor, like that of the German humorists, is obviously too deeply rooted in the local community, and penetrates at times so far into the Yankee soul that the German reader can follow it only if he has lived many years in the States.[29] On the other hand, our German critics are almost one in feeling that Mark Twain found the complete expression for Yankee humor, that his humor was so deep and broad that he awakens laughter

[29] Gottberg, *Velhagen & Klasings Monatshefte*, June, 1910.

even when one is unable to understand him completely. He is the only American humorist, as the young Danish novelist Johannes von Jensen remarks, "who is so universal and who has such an enlightened conception of the nature of humor that he succeeded in establishing just as great a reputation abroad as at home."[30]

As in the preceding periods, our German commentators devote much attention to a consideration of the nature of American humor and of Mark Twain's humor as the most realistic and most characteristic embodiment of its spirit. American humor, in their view, derives its significance from the fact that compared with other literary fields, where American authors show the influence of European culture, it is the one original literary product of American culture that is a distinct development out of the life of the Yankee—the one sphere of literary endeavor which presents something unavailable elsewhere. Here, it is contended, the German reader is able to gain a deep insight into the innermost soul of the American people, and to breathe and feel America. Paul Landau's remarks in this connection are quite informative. He points out that Poe and Hawthorne are only "slightly American, but deeply rooted in German romanticism and the English novel"; that the practical wisdom of an Emerson and the natural poetry of a Thoreau "sounded familiar to the European reader" and only slightly varied from his own patterns; that even in the poetry of Walt Whitman, in whom "primitive greatness and creative force resounded from a new world," the Germans found information only "about the heroes of the Civil War, but nothing of the contemporary Yankee." The content of Bret Harte's work he finds interesting and original, but "in technique influenced by the great narrators of all times," and artistically it seems to him much more closely related to Maupassant's style than to that of one of the contemporary Americans. Even today, Landau holds, much that is poetically worth while is produced in America, but it likewise

[30] Jensen was widely known as a satirist and great *Welthumorist*. He was strongly Americanized, and wrote many newspaper articles on President Theodore Roosevelt. The Negro question held a particular fascination for him. His comments and evaluation of Mark Twain were translated by Julia Koppel of Hamburg and appeared in the *Frankfurter Zeitung* of April 26, 1910. Jensen was one of the contemporary European critics who demanded a more serious interpretation of Mark Twain as an author.

is influenced by Zola and Bourget, as well as by Maeterlinck and d'Annunzio.[31]

In their discussion of Mark Twain's humor, our critics (with one notable exception)[32] deliberately avoid defining the term "humor." They confine themselves in the main to the citation of various characteristics which resolve themselves, under analysis, into the component elements of his humor. His early humor, these critics are wont to point out, is dependent upon forced verbal witticisms and monstrous exaggerations. His more mature humor, on the other hand, avoids the local, the verbal witticism, and the eccentric climaxes; it studies the weaknesses and the daily life of mankind, and brings all into correct relationship to the historical and cultural background of its time. "Grotesque exaggeration" constitutes the real essence of his humor; but while some sensitive natures take exception to this particular characteristic, others defend and justify it as a legitimate means of expressing the infinite or as a method of satisfying the enormous dimensions required by the telescopic nature of Mark Twain as revealed in his life and in the play of his imagination. In this connection our German critics do not fail to discover and emphasize the stylistic means by which he produces his drastic effects. They stress particularly his inexhaustible and startlingly effective use of hyperbole and his skill in presenting an antithesis of over-powering humorous force.

It is also interesting to note that a minority of those critics who attempted to analyze his humor judged it according to standards set up by German æsthetic theory. The findings of two of these are important by way of contrast and supplement in the effort to explain Mark Twain's humor, and are therefore deserving of special consideration. Interpreting Mark Twain's humor in the light of Jean Paul's conception,[33] Rudolf Fürst,[34] author, literary

[31] *Allgemeine Zeitung, Beilage* (Munich), November 30, 1905; *B.Z.am Mittag,* April 22, 1910.

[32] Hugo Eick, *März* (Munich), May, 1910. Eick, a student under Brandl and for years an instructor in a commercial institute in Bremen, defines humor broadly as an expression of a disposition, a constitutional characteristic, an ethical *Gesamtanschauung*. With this explanation as the basis of his discussion, he seeks to illustrate it in the printed works of Mark Twain. He traces the utilitarian progress of the American people and shows how Mark Twain's humor reflects the very essence of that American life which he personally experienced and embodied.

[33] "Humor," says Jean Paul, "as the inversion of the sublime, does not destroy the

historian, critic, and a frequent contributor to important German scholarly journals, points out that the American shows that contempt for life which the German author demands as an indispensable requisite of humor: he grasps the mad world, he says, in its totality, he disintegrates it in isolated phenomena, and he exalts the lowly and debases the exalted in order to destroy both. In many examples our critic shows how Mark Twain's humor attacks with biting satire the vexations and burdens of daily domestic life and the obnoxious practices of public life.[35] The German reader, Fürst maintains, is willing to follow Mark Twain whenever he elevates *das Kleine,* but is filled with resentment whenever he attacks the exalted and the sublime. He is not inclined, for example, to expose to the satiric darts of a humorist the delights and pleasures of Alpine sports, or the intense joy of a sunrise in the mountains, or an intelligent and appreciative joy in the old masters. In this respect he finds that the German, who is historically sensitive and naïve in his enjoyment, cannot and will not keep pace with the practically minded American. On the other hand, Leon Kellner,[36] at the time professor of English philology and literature in the University of Czernowitz,[37] deprecates the tendency of some German critics to judge American humor, and specifically Mark Twain's humor, by German standards. The German reader, he warns, should not for a moment think of applying Jean Paul's, Friedrich Schlegel's, or Vischer's definition to Ameri-

individual, but the finite, through the contrast with the idea. For it no isolated folly exists, but only folly and a mad world; unlike the ordinary buffoon with his sly shafts, it singles out no isolated folly; it humiliates the exalted, not like the parody, in order to set the lowly beside it; and it exalts the lowly, not like irony, in order to set the exalted beside it, and thus to destroy them both, for in the presence of the infinite everything is alike and is nothing."

[34] *Vossische Zeitung,* 1905, Nr. 561. Fürst was a native Bohemian. His interest in the development of German-Bohemian literature led to studies of August Gottlieb Meissner, Stifter, and Moritz Reich. His reputation was greatly enhanced by his literary-historical treatises on Keller, Raimund, and Halm. One of his best-known works is his Heine biography.

[35] Instances of these abuses are the coarse tone of the press, the jurist and bureaucrats, the obstructionists and pedants, the pompous police and detectives, the eccentric passion of collectors, etc.

[36] Professor Kellner's remarkable familiarity, not only with Amerian literature, but also with America's historic past, is shown in his *Geschichte der nordamerikanischen Literatur,* published at Leipsic in 1914. He set himself the task of acquainting Germans with the characteristic features of the literature of our country.

[37] The city of Czernowitz is in the former Austrian crown land of Bukowina.

can humor, nor should he even attempt to seek the comparatively simple qualities demanded of humor in Lazarus' *Leben der Seele*,[38] for example, in the story of the jumping frog or the scene where Tom Sawyer obtains the prize for Bible study. The reader, he argues, is of course free to establish in Mark Twain's jokes the metaphysical contradiction between idea and reality; but it is unnecessary to look for deeper explanations wherever the author produces gross effects by gross means.

In reviewing the evidence that has been thus adduced for the five years from 1905 to 1910, certain general conclusions may be drawn. In the first place, the repeated publication of the *Sketches*, which apparently did not diminish in popularity, and of *The Adventures of Tom Sawyer* and *The Adventures of Huckleberry Finn*, indicates that the German publishers were acceding more and more to the demands of the consuming public. The public preference for these works, however, is not adequately reflected in the critical literature of these years. Although the sifting process generally begins only after a writer has died and thus has begun, so to speak, his journey through the ages, there was a tendency even before Mark Twain's death to evaluate his multifarious writings. German critical opinion is unanimous in conceding preeminence to the *Sketches*. Pötzl, for example, feels that these small humoresques, written in the tone of the backwoods newspapers, actually laid the foundation and prepared the way for the success of Mark Twain's larger works. As a wholesome remedy against melancholy and ill-humor, he accords these "amiable trifles" a value that will assure them validity in the years to come. The *Skizzenbuch* and *Reisebilder* alone would, in his judgment, promise immortality to Mark Twain.[39]

---

[38] "The spirit of humor," says Lazarus, "sees itself and its actual life remote from the idea, powerless to attain their ends and its intent, consequently subdued and crushed and often condemned to the despairing derision of self-contempt; and, on the other hand, uplifted and purified by the consciousness of possessing and dominating the idea (and the infinite) despite everything, and of presenting and exemplifying it, though in ever so imperfect a form, and of being one with it in its deeper essence, if only through the knowledge gained from it and the painful sense of imperfection." Translation by Julia Franklin in Leon Kellner's *American Literature*. New York: Doubleday, Page & Co., 1915, p. 205.

[39] Eduard Lipton (*Wiener Deutsches Tagblatt*, November 30, 1905) shares this view.

On the other hand, our critics are divided on the ranking and permanent validity of the other works. Saager, for example, feels that *Tom Sawyer*, *Huckleberry Finn*, and *Pudd'nhead Wilson* entitle Mark Twain to recognition as a "Dichter" who may claim a place in the literature of the world.[40] Some critics are inclined to those works which are purely entertaining,[41] and consequently best known, those in which the author reveals an unusual fertility of imagination; others lean to those with a permanent cultural and historical value;[42] while still others seek the most significant expression of his genius in the works of travel and description.[43]

As in former years, a large portion of the material about Mark Twain is purely informative in nature, and is devoted primarily to a consideration of the subject matter of the author's works and to his personal career. Of particular importance, however, are those journals which contributed toward a fuller understanding of Mark Twain by bringing to the forefront the widely varying attitude of the critics towards *Is Shakespeare Dead?*.

The tributes called forth by the author's seventieth anniversary in 1905 and by his death in 1910 give documentary evidence that Mark Twain occupied a unique place in German affections. They confine themselves, on the whole, to a presentation of events in his colorful career and to a concise discussion of his work. His popularity is accepted as an established fact, and an attempt is made to explain its basis. A number of factors—personal, commercial, and literary—are mentioned, not one of which, however, furnishes a complete explanation in itself. The one complements the other, but all the factors taken together contribute to an understanding of Mark Twain's sustained reputation in Germany.

If there was any particular phase of Mark Twain's life, a life aptly characterized as a "zigzag career," that left an especial im-

---

[40] *Hamburger Nachrichten*, November 29, 1905.

[41] Cf. also Diederich, *Tägliche Rundschau*, November 29, 1905, p. 1118; Jensen, *Frankfurter Zeitung*, April 26, 1910.

[42] These are held to be such works as *Life on the Mississippi*, *A Connecticut Yankee*, *Joan of Arc*, *The Prince and the Pauper*, and *Puddn'head Wilson*. Bratter (*B.Z. am Mittag*, April 22, 1910) is inclined to accept the last, with its emphatic condemnation of slavery and its cultural picture of the Southwest in the 1830's, as Mark Twain's masterpiece.

[43] For example, *The Innocents Abroad*, *A Tramp Abroad*, or *Roughing It*.

pression on the minds of the critics in these years, it was his activity in the field of business. They are generally agreed that the humorist Mark Twain never forgot, even for a day, what the author Mark Twain owed to the business man Clemens. His ambitions for success in business, they contend, were not less sincere than for success as an author. Though his career as a business man met with failure, his career as an author gained from this association. His unmerited misfortune gained for him the sympathy of his countrymen and made it possible for him to pay his debts and to accumulate another fortune. In prosperity and in adversity the characteristic that distinguishes Mark Twain's nature most deeply is enormous vitality.

Of this period it cannot be said that the critical discussion of Mark Twain as the typical representative of American humor supplements greatly that of the preceding years. American humor is unanimously accepted as a peculiarly American growth, interpreted in the light of American social and political conditions. The characterization of American humor and consequently of Mark Twain's humor remains very much the same; its chief features are a definite pose and, stylistically, a sort of cool, objective irony, self-evident exaggeration, and an amazing absurdity.

The view that had formerly been widespread in Germany, that of Mark Twain as a mere buffoon and a jester, the embodiment of the coarse-grained and baroque caprices of the Yankee, still finds considerable support in these years. There are those who still hold to the argument that his purpose was merely to amuse the world; although these critics admit that he was a satirist and a delineator of American life, they nevertheless feel that his satire is without teeth, that it does not destroy, that it has mere laughter as its sole objective. These writers resent any tendency that would place Mark Twain on a par, or even compare him, with Jean Paul, Dickens, or Claude Tillier.

There is, however, still another group of critics which is convinced that Mark Twain has based his claims upon humor alone and thereby closed the path to posthumous fame. There was a time, these maintain, when Mark Twain was *the* humorist, the world-famous humorist; but with his death his humor has become superannuated and obsolete. Yet even the proponents of this view admit that, regardless of the fate of his work, his name will not altogether vanish, for he is one of the great men of the world, one of those who was greater than his works, one to whom the world cannot afford to become indifferent. There is, indeed, a dominant feeling among the German critics that when the period to which Mark Twain belongs and the types which he has exposed with his wit have grown pale in memory, posterity will not forget that he was one of those who paved the way to a new time and to a new people.

IV

GERMAN INTEREST IN AMERICAN APPRAISALS
1910-1918

Responsive mood of German publishers, 1910-1918——Archibald Henderson
——Charles Alphonso Smith——Summary.

There is a modest measure of evidence in the eight years that followed Mark Twain's death, from 1910 to 1918, the end of the World War, to confirm the belief that the American humorist did not forfeit prestige among German readers. An analysis of the publications of his works in these years indicates that German publishers still found it expedient in spite of adverse economic conditions to supplement their series of foreign authors with at least one or more volumes by the American author. Among the numerous publishers who added, for the first time, Mark Twain volumes—for example, the Neues Literarisches Institut of Stuttgart,[1] Jaeger of Leipsic,[2] Heilbrunn & Co. of Berlin,[3] the "Verein für Verbreitung guter Schriften" in Zürich[4]—that of Hesse & Becker is particularly deserving of attention. Sometime after 1910 this firm expressed its growing confidence in the unique value of Mark Twain's writings by issuing a three-volume edition[5] of his

---

[1] In 1911 this firm added *Tom Sawyer als Detektiv, wie es Huck Finn erzählt* as the sixth volume of a series of twelve volumes known as "Saturn. Illustrierte Universal-Bibliothek." This edition was an unusually cheap one, each volume being priced at twenty-five pfennigs. The illustrations for the Mark Twain volume, as for the entire series, were done by Theodor Volz.

[2] Jaeger incorporated Mark Twain's *How I Edited an Agricultural Paper* into the twelfth volume (1912) of a series entitled "Sammlung englischer und französischer Autoren." Among the selections from American humor which made up this volume were Washington Irving's *Rip van Winkle* and Bret Harte's *Baby Sylvester*.

[3] In 1912 this firm issued a series of some twenty-seven volumes, known as "Albert Bonniers 30-Pfenning-Bücherei." Among the many authors included were Kipling, Poe, Strindberg, and Mark Twain. Vol. XIV contained Mark Twain's *Der berüchtigte (springende) Frosch der Grafschaft Calaveras und andere Erzählungen.*

[4] This firm selected Mark Twain's *Die Verschwörung von Fort Trumbull. Das Todeslos,* a pamphlet of some fifty-three pages, for its ninety-fifth number (1913).

[5] Vol. I contained *Humoristische Skizzen. Reisebilder* and a frontispiece; Vol. II, *Tom Sawyers Abenteuer und Streiche, Die Millionpfundnote und andere Erzählungen;* and Vol. III, *Huckleberry Finns Abenteuer und Fahrten. Tot oder Lebendig und andere Erzählungen.* Vol. I also brought a very short biographical sketch of Mark Twain's life and an appraisal by Dr. Ludwig Fürstenwerth, lecturer and critic. Fürstenwerth's interest in humor as a specific phase of literature led him to edit

works as part of a series known significantly as "Romane der Weltliteratur," following it the next year with a six-volume edition of his *Auserwählte Werke*.[6] It took cognizance of the increasing popularity of *Tom Sawyers Abenteuer und Streiche* and *Huckleberry Finns Abenteuer und Fahrten*,[7] and for the convenience of the German readers offered these in one volume. The preparation of *The Prince and the Pauper*[8] and *The Adventures of Tom Sawyer*[9] for school instruction testifies, in some measure, to the growing conviction that Mark Twain's wholesome and amiable humor contained appropriate and productive reading for German youth. Although Tauchnitz issued only three volumes[10] during these years, Lutz continued without interruption his efforts to popularize Mark Twain, not so much by new additions as by repeated issues of the works which had already appeared with his imprint. The six volumes[11] of *Mark Twains ausgewählte humor-*

and publish (in 1912) two volumes of selections from humorous literature "old and new" under the title *Vom köstlichen Humor.*

[6] The content of these volumes is identical with that of the three-volume edition which appeared in the preceding year. Four of these volumes also appeared in "Hesses Volksbücherei": Vol. I (Nos. 649 & 650 of "Hesses Volksbücherei"), *Humoristische Skizzen;* Vol. II (Nos. 651-654), *Tom Sawyers Abenteuer und Streiche;* Vol. III (Nos. 655-656), *Reisebilder;* and Vol. IV (Nos. 657-660), *Huckleberry Finns Abenteuer und Fahrten.*

[7] These two romances also found publication as *Die Abenteuer des Tom Sawyer und Huckleberry Finn* in Vol. V of the "Singer-Bücher," a series of seven volumes which contained contributions by such writers as Balzac, E.T.A. Hoffman, Selma Lagerlöf, Maupassant, Poe, and Strindberg. Part I was translated by Ulrich Johannsen, part II by Marie Schloss. The illustrations were by E. Hirth.

[8] Incorporated into "Freytags Sammlung französischer und englischer Schriftsteller" and into "Velhagen & Klasings Sammlung französischer und englischer Schulausgaben. English Authors." The Freytag abridged edition was arranged by Rudolf Richter, the Velhagen & Klasing by F. Roebbelen. Each contained an introduction with a brief illuminating survey of Mark Twain's life and works.

[9] Velhagen & Klasing added this volume to its list of English authors in 1914. This edition was prepared by H. Perschman, professor at the Oberlyzeum in Osnabrück, and likewise contained an introduction dealing with Mark Twain's life.

[10] In 1916 appeared a copyright edition of *Tom Sawyer Detective as told by Huck Finn* in "Tauchnitz Pocket Library" (Vol. LXXV), and a volume of *Sketches,* Series I, in the "English Textbooks" (Vol. XXXII). A second series of *Sketches* appeared later in 1918 in "Tauchnitz Pocket Library" (Vol. LXXXVIII).

[11] The following tabulation will at least give the reader an idea of the Lutz circulation to the end of the War. By 1918 Vol. I, *Tom Sawyers Streiche und Abenteuer,* reached its thirty-fourth printing; Vol. II, *Abenteuer und Fahrten des Huckleberry Finn,* its thirtieth; Vol. III, *Skizzenbuch,* its twenty-sixth; by 1914 Vol. IV, *Auf dem Mississippi. Lehr- und Wanderjahre,* its twentieth printing; by 1918 Vol. V, *Im Gold- und Silberland,* its nineteenth; and by 1912 Vol. VI, *Reisebilder,* its twenty-first.

istische Schriften, which Lutz first published in 1892; the illustrated edition of the same six volumes,[12] which made its first appearance in 1898; and the six volumes[13] of the *Neue Folge humoristischer Schriften,* first issued in 1903 in the Lutz Verlag, all experienced repeated printings.

A glance, however, at the critical material on Mark Twain made available to the German reader in these years does not reveal a similar responsiveness. A careful examination shows that no outstanding German writer had anything substantial or helpful to say about him. There were, to be sure, a few articles[14] of a purely informative character, and there were reviews in various educational journals,[15] which, though they kept an interest in Mark

[12] Vol. I reached its twenty-first printing in 1918; Vol. II its seventeenth and Vol. III its twelfth by that time; Vol. IV its tenth in 1909; Vol. V its eleventh in 1912; and Vol. VI its eleventh in 1914.

[13] Vol. I, *Tom Sawyers neue Abenteuer (Tom Sawyer im Luftballon. Tom, der kleine Detektiv),* reached its twelfth printing in 1915; Vol. II, *Querkopf Wilson,* its ninth in 1917; Vols. III and IV, *Meine Reise um die Welt,* their ninth in 1918; and Vol. VI, *Wie Hadleyburg verderbt wurde,* its eighth printing in 1913.

It is practically impossible to determine accurately the years in which the various works were reprinted.

[14] It must be kept in mind that neither Mark Twain's *Autobiography* nor Albert Bigelow Paine's biography of Mark Twain was translated into German. Therefore articles dealing with the facts of the author's life are worthy of inspection in so far as they assist in rounding out the picture of Mark Twain for the German reader. See Brix Förster, *Allgemeine Zeitung* (Munich), May 21, 1910, for a short résumé of those selections from Mark Twain's *Autobiography* which had appeared in 1906 and 1907 (seven issues) in the *North American Review;* the *Bayerische Kurier,* August 8, 1912, for a discussion of Mark Twain's sojourn in Heidelberg and Munich; *Kieler Zeitung,* October 28, 1916, for a translation of Gustav Thalberg's discussion of Mark Twain and his models for the characters in *Tom Sawyer* and *Huckleberry Finn.* In this connection attention should be directed particularly to an article that is of more than passing interest, not only to the German but also to the American reader. In the *Zeitschrift für französischen und englischen Unterricht* (XVI, 358) H. Engel of Charlottenburg recalls a lecture Mark Twain delivered, perhaps in 1890, at a Girls' School in Berlin. Although a large part of the audience apparently enjoyed it, our commentator and his friends were irritated. The astounding fact is that Engel found the very striking characteristics which amused thousands of people at his lectures—namely, the nasal tone of his voice and the slow, dragging drawl—objectionable. It is highly probable that he was placed in an unpleasant mood by the introductory remarks of the director of the school, an apparently well-known and excellent *Neuphilologe,* who thanked Mark Twain for the opportunity he had given them of glancing into the mental workshop of a great man and who characterized the evening as a "milepost" for the further development of modern philology along new paths. There were no doubt many German critics who agreed with Engel that this was extravagant praise, and supported him in his plea for a more objective judgment.

[15] Cf. *Frauenbildung,* XIV (1915), 349; *Englische Studien,* XLIX (1916), 467 f.;

Twain alive, nevertheless are lacking in critical insight. And yet there is impressive proof that German thought was quietly following the progressive development of the Mark Twain vogue in America as well as in Germany. In this connection the *Deutsche Revue* is noteworthy for its efforts to familiarize the German reader with American critical opinion of Mark Twain. In February of 1911 this journal[16] published a discussion in German by the American scholar, Archibald Henderson. Henderson was at that time professor of pure mathematics at the University of North Carolina, and in the years to come was to distinguish himself with numerous publications in scientific, literary, and historical periodicals. His interpretations of Ibsen, Shaw, and other European dramatists were to earn him recognition in the annals of American literary criticism. He was personally acquainted with Mark Twain, and this fact alone, we may assume, gave importance in the minds of his readers to his treatment of the author, whom he discusses as moralist, philosopher, sociologist, and reformer. German critics, as we have pointed out in preceding chapters, had discovered the moralist and the philosopher in Mark Twain, but it had been invariably a merely superficial recognition. At no time had any of these commentators entered on a serious and exhaustive analysis of Mark Twain's work in this direction.

In the first place Henderson attempts to show that humor does not form the principal basis of Mark Twain's fame. This was not altogether new to German readers. The critic, Hugo Eick, had expressed a similar view. In his judgment the rôle of humorist is neither the most significant nor the most interesting trait in Mark Twain; it is only the best known form of a literary type which incorporates the entire history of the American people. The same idea had been expressed five years earlier in a feuilleton by Phillipp Berges, journalist, dramatist, and novelist of "das litterarische Hamburg."[17]

Henderson now sets forth at length the theory of the moral significance of Mark Twain's work. As a prelude to his argument

---

and the *Zeitschrift für französischen und englischen Unterricht,* XVI (1917), 70 f., 171-183, 357 f.

[16] XXXVI, 189-205.

[17] Cf. *Norddeutsche Allgemeine Zeitung* (Berlin), November 30, 1905.

he points out that it is impossible to name one great international figure in the entire history of literature whose fame rests solely upon the basis of humor. The very greatest of humorists—Rabelais, La Fontaine, Cervantes, and Molière—owe their world-wide recognition to "a breadth of philosophy, a depth of sadness, or a profundity of pathos" inherent in their humor. The presence of these qualities in Mark Twain's art, intensified in later years by a serious spirit, a grim irony, and an intense passion for justice and truth, should entitle him to serious consideration as an out-standing moralist and philosopher. This basic seriousness and moral conviction Henderson sees most strikingly reflected in *Huckleberry Finn,* in the significant passage in which Huck strug-gles with his conscience over "the knotty problem of his moral responsibility for compassing Jim's emancipation." It gives definite evidence, as our critic aptly puts it, of Mark Twain's "preoccupa-tion with the workings of human conscience in the unsophisticated mind," and documents his conviction that "Huck was justified in his courageous decision."

Turning to an analysis of Mark Twain's favorite themes as a moralist, Henderson calls attention to one of the most suggestive, "the subject of prevarication."[18] He shows, by numerous examples, how "its utility, its convenience, and its consequences" took the form of stories and epigrams. Mark Twain's method is "humorous inversion"; that is, he tells a story in which ethical ideas are so ludicrously twisted that the right moral principle springs to light

[18] Henderson relates what he calls "Mark Twain's most humorous anecdote," based, of course, on the subject of prevarication. It is mentioned here in order to show the difficulties that are encountered in translating from one language into the other. Meeting an exceedingly old darky in the South who claimed that he crossed the Delaware with Washington, Mark Twain asked, "Were you with Washington when he took that hack at the cherry tree?" The darky, realizing that his pride was at stake, replied: "Lord, boss, I was dar. In cose I was. I was with Marse George at dat very time. In fac—I done druv dat hack myself!" An American will im-mediately recognize the dual meaning of that one word, "hack," upon which the entire point of the story hangs. But the German translator of Henderson's article presumably did not. Mark Twain's question he renders with, "Waren Sie bei Wash-ington, als er die vielbesprochene Axt bei dem Kirschbaum ergriff?" And the darky's reply, "Ja, ja, ich dabei gewesen. Gewiss, ich dabei. Ich gewesen bei Marse George gerade damals. Ja, ja, ich selbst geholen den Axt!" This is, of course, merely one example. But we can readily understand, perhaps, why *Huckleberry Finn,* with its dialect, did not receive its just measure of recognition in Germany.

by contrast. Equally vital for Mark Twain's recognition as a moralist is the distinction he was fond of drawing between "theoretical and practical morals." Theoretical morals, our critic quotes Mark Twain as saying, are those which one gets "from good books and from the pulpit,"—the sort that one gets "into the head, but not into the heart"; practical morals are those acquired through the commission of all kinds of crimes. In this connection Mark Twain, "the humorous moralist," suggests an interesting contrast to Bernard Shaw, "the ethical thinker."

However, the primary source of support for Henderson's contention that the American writer was not only "a supreme artist" but also "an eminent and distinctive moralist," is in the larger works. Four of these are analyzed at some length. The first, *The Man that Corrupted Hadleyburg,* is characterized as a "masterpiece," a profound parable with a grimly ironic conclusion, a moral lesson pure and simple, animated by "its brilliantly original ethical suggestiveness" and by "its illuminating reflection of human nature and its graciously relieving humor." The second, *In Defense of Harriet Shelley,* is said to give evidence of "an act of high courage and nobility" and of the author's sympathy for the oppressed, the weak, and the defenseless. The third, *Joan of Arc,* serves similarly to emphasize Mark Twain's respect and sympathy for the life and conduct of the simple maid of Orleans. The fourth work which Henderson lists is the story *Was it Heaven or Hell?,* with its attack upon "rigidly formal Puritanism," which is set over against human nature, and upon the tragic result of adherence "to the letter instead of to the spirit of the moral law." All these works, in Henderson's judgment, are "essential vindications of the moral principle"; but *Was it Heaven or Hell?* and *The Man that Corrupted Hadleyburg* in particular give forceful expression to "that same transvaluation of current moral values which marks the age of Nietzsche and Ibsen, Tolstoy and Shaw."

Of far more decisive character is the discussion which revolves about Mark Twain as a sociologist. According to Henderson, this is the function by which he attains "supreme title to distinction as a great writer." Defining sociology by implication as "the highest sphere of thought, embracing religion, philosophy, morality, and even humor," our American critic finds the most noble expression of this in the author's attitude toward slavery. Mark Twain's unconditional acceptance of slavery as an established institution was a matter of Southern tradition. His subsequent rejection of it as "unjust, inhuman and indefensible" was the inevitable result of his own experiences and of his accumulated knowledge of life. The fact that he wrote his books when slavery was a thing of the past enabled him to judge the situation objectively. His object, Henderson declares, was not that of the fanatical reformer, "warped with prejudice and fired by animosity." His aim was not "polemic, but artistic," and in its presentation was the achievement of a remarkable sociologist. Henderson cites particularly *Huckleberry Finn* and *Life on the Mississippi,* with their vivid pictures of feuds, of "the lordly life of the pilots," of "the lawless, picturesque, semi-barbarous life of the river," in support of his view that Mark Twain is a writer who is primarily a great artist, but—unconsciously—also a true sociologist. The defining quality of a true sociologist is "the faculty of penetrating national and racial disguises, and going directly to the heart of the human problem." Mark Twain's essay *Concerning the Jews,* which our critic terms "a masterpiece of impartial interpretation"; his "comprehension of French and German racial traits"; his "analysis of the situation in South Africa"; his "interpretation of American democracy[19] and mirroring of the national ideals"; and his study of Christian Science, "a sociological study of religious fanaticism, comprehensive in its psychological analysis of national and racial traits"—these are a few of the impressive proofs which, as he believes, amply demonstrate Mark Twain's "remarkable and profound" talents as a social and racial critic, and justify the conclusion that "Mark Twain possessed this faculty in a supreme degree."

[19] Henderson stresses in particular "the dream of democracy." *The Prince and the Pauper,* for example, with its "successful substitution of the commoner for the king," becomes a "symbolic legend of democracy and the equality of man." *A Yankee at the Court of King Arthur* our critic interprets as "a remarkable brief for democracy and the brotherhood of man." Henderson, however, emphasizes the point, which had not escaped the attention of some German critics, that even though Mark Twain lost faith in humanity itself, he never lost faith in democracy, and to the very end of his life fought on behalf of "equality and the welfare of the average man."

Of importance at this particular time for its substantial contribution toward the moulding of a serious and well-informed opinion of Mark Twain in Germany was the critical appraisement by Charles Alphonso Smith, an American scholar of some distinction. Smith (1864-1924) was himself of German ancestry. A superb raconteur and a very able and stimulating lecturer, he held professorships at Louisiana State University[20] (1893-1902), and at the University of North Carolina (1902-1909), where he became the first dean of its graduate school. He reached the fullness of his powers and popularity as first Edgar Allan Poe Professor of English at the University of Virginia (1909-1917). In 1910-1911 he was granted a leave of absence to serve as Roosevelt Professor of American History and Institutions at the University of Berlin. Here he conducted a seminar on Poe and delivered a number of lectures in German on American literature. These included appreciations of Benjamin Franklin, Thomas Jefferson, Washington Irving, "Idealism in American literature," James Fenimore Cooper, "American poetry," Poe, Emerson, Longfellow, Whitman, and others. Smith's power lay in his delightful personality and in a psychological instinct that enabled him to communicate his enthusiasm vividly to others. It may be assumed that these qualities also had their effect on the educated group of hearers and readers in Germany with whom he came into contact and that they were not without effect in awakening a keener interest in Mark Twain.

In a simple and concise manner[21] Smith evaluates Mark Twain's work as an expression of an unusually strong feeling for contrasts, not contrasts in general, but principally such contrasts as he ob-

[20] Smith's scholarly productions included *Repetition and Parallelism in English Verse* (1894); *An Old English Grammar* (1896); *Studies in English Syntax* (1906); *An English-German Conversation Book* (1902); grammars for school use; *What can Literature do for me?*, perhaps his most widely circulated book; and *O. Henry Biography* (1916), perhaps his most ambitious literary work. He was active also as the founder and editor of *Studies in Philology* (published at the University of North Carolina). For years he was on the editorial staff of the *Library of Southern Literature* (17 volumes, 1907-1923).

[21] Smith's lecture, "Mark Twain und der amerikanische Humor," was incorporated later into his book *Die amerikanische Literatur, Vorlesung gehalten an der Königlichen Friedrich-Wilhelms-Universität zu Berlin.* The book appeared as Vol. II of the "Bibliothek der amerikanischen Kulturgeschichte," edited by Dr. Nicholas Murray Butler and Dr. Wilhelm Paszkowski, director of the "Akademische Auskunftsstelle an der Universität Berlin" (Berlin: Weidmannsche Buchhandlung, 1912).

served minutely with his own keen eyes. Among the most dominant factors that served to develop that tendency were the period and the place of his birth. This background, Smith contends, assumes greater importance because Missouri had entered the Union as a slave state and was for a time the most western of all the states. In this frontier position it received through constantly increasing traffic on the Mississippi a population which was perhaps the most rapidly growing and the most representative that came to any state in the Union in those days.

Every class was represented—poor and rich, good and bad, educated and ignorant, slave and freeman. Such an environment presented "dramatic character contrasts in social position, contrasts of conservatism and radicalism, of nationalism and provincialism, of humor and pathos," in short, contrasts such as had rarely existed before in America. There was hardly an American author, our critic observes, who had the good fortune to be surrounded by such numerous opportunities to view human life in all its strangeness and particularities as Mark Twain.

In common with many Germans, Smith holds the opinion that Mark Twain's ultimate purpose was not to amuse the world but to express the truth in such a way as he himself found it. With this as the basic conception, our critic then traces the development of the idea of contrast in the various works of the author. The first definite attempt at evolving a clearly defined contrast he finds in *The Adventures of Tom Sawyer* (1876). Here the contrast between Tom and Huck is that between an individual who sees life through sentimental books and a person who does not concern himself about books, but in every embarrassment depends solely upon his own, sound, human reason. Thus in Tom we have the romanticist; in Huck, the realist. Gradually the character of Tom Sawyer shows itself not only the type of a boy's character but the symbol of "the spirit of the age of King Arthur," the symbol of the "exaggerated and the romantic,"—in a word, the symbol of the influence of Walter Scott.[22] While the character of Huck shows

[22] Mark Twain's dislike of Scott is not shared by Smith. As a Southerner, Smith defends Scott and would like to see his influence encouraged on the ground that the industrial age requires an appeal to the nobler qualities of the mind and heart. In his opinion, there is no author better equipped to do that than Scott. A democracy

a development, that of Tom remains the same to the end. He is, indeed, as Smith sees him, hardly a figure of flesh and blood, but merely a concept, a point of view. In *A Tramp Abroad* (1880) our critic sees the contrast between European and American life. He concedes that the American side is usually suppressed but finds that it is nevertheless quietly and persistently pursued. In fact, he is inclined to interpret the work, in the things that are mentioned and in those that are omitted, as a reflection on American as well as European life.[23] In *The Prince and the Pauper* (1882) Smith sees the author's attention focused, not on the story, but on the possibility of a contrast between a prince who lives as a beggar and a beggar who lives as a prince. In *Life on the Mississippi* (1883) he notes the contrast in the kaleidoscopic life on the great river before and after the war. For *A Connecticut Yankee* (1889) Smith suggests the title *Bridgeport in Connecticut in the year 1879 vs. Camelot in England in the year 528, or Tom Sawyer overthrown by Huck Finn.* The introduction of modern enterprises at the Court of King Arthur serves to heighten the contrast. *Puddn'head Wilson* (1893) is in reality the old story of *The Prince and the Pauper* transplanted to the State of Missouri of 1830. Here we have the antithesis of freedom and slavery. In *The Personal Recollections of Joan of Arc* (1896) Smith points to the contrast between the maiden herself and the century in which she lived. Mark Twain indicates in the foreword quite clearly that this had attracted him to the theme. The contrast between the kindliness of Joan and the surrounding baseness develops, not in a humorous atmosphere, but rather in one of moral indignation. In Mark Twain's last work, *Extracts from Captain Stormfield's Visit to Heaven* (1909), Smith finds the contrast in the conventional, Sunday-school conception of heaven with the heaven which Captain Stormfield actually finds.

Having thus established his position with reference to the purpose and spirit of the author, Smith moves on to a consideration of Mark Twain's technique. Humor, he explains, was the means he employed to make these contrasts as vivid for others as they

---

must be reminded continually that not all chivalry is to be identified with false chivalry, nor all feeling with sentimentality. Smith, *op. cit.*, p. 322.

[23] *Ibid.*, pp. 323 f.

were to him. As evidence that this humor is also typically American, he advances three arguments. In the first place, it is applied, not for its own sake, but for the thought and feeling underlying it. In examining Mark Twain's humor he considers it imperative to keep constantly in mind that a man living during the periods before and after 1861-1865 lived really in two worlds and two centuries, that the social and political changes were both tragic and humorous, depending entirely upon one's interpretation. Mark Twain could have chosen the tragic approach, but the humorous served his purpose better. Comparing Mark Twain with the great American humorists who preceded him, Smith finds that their humor is identical in that it had a purpose. Franklin, he says, used humor "not to tell incidental jokes, but to clarify generalizations, to emphasize convictions, to give popular form to a difficult chapter in philosophy." With Irving, humor is the servant of pathos. In the works of Oliver Wendell Holmes, humor (or better—wit) expresses itself in epigrams and aphorisms; it is local, capricious, and fragmentary, and is not related to the humor of situation—it is always in the service of a well-disciplined intellect. In the hands of Lowell, it is a weapon in defense of the fatherland. Mark Twain's humor is likewise humor with a purpose, the secret of which must be sought, not in abstract theories, but in the character of the man himself and in the changing milieu in which he lived. American humor as a whole Smith aptly compares to an allegory: on the surface it is simple entertainment, but below the surface it is a criticism of life.

Taking up his second argument, Smith finds Mark Twain's humor typically American because it makes extensive use of exaggeration. Exaggeration, in fact, plays a more effective rôle in the writings of Mark Twain than in those of any other American humorist. His natural love of contrast, his numerous experiences in the South and the West, his lack of academic training, his travels, his successes and failures are all factors in his tendency towards humorous exaggeration. He defends Mark Twain against the criticism of those who condemn his love of exaggeration and declares that much so-called exaggeration in American humor is not exaggeration at all, but only a bold, unconventional attempt to express the "inexpressible." Parts of *Captain Stormfield's Visit to Heaven*, he explains, are not an exaggeration, but only an attempt to find a formula for the infinite. It is impossible to exaggerate the infinite; one can only approach it. Mark Twain's humor and American humor, in general, he concludes, is frequently of this nature.

Finally, Smith holds Mark Twain's humor typically American because it reproduces the social and political conditions in which it had its origin. On the basis of Ernst Elster's *Prinzipien der Literaturwissenschaft*,[24] which he quotes for its categories of humor,[25] he assigns Mark Twain's humor to the socio-political category, finding evidence in frequent juxtaposition of the conventional and rude reality, religion and morality, sentimentality and true feeling, individualism and institutionalism. Since Mark Twain was entirely the product of neither individualism nor institutionalism, but stood on the boundary line between the two, our critic labels him "a literary frontiersman," "a historian of the individual" who seeks to adapt himself to the surrounding social and political conditions. It is this contrast between the individual —the creation of nature—and the institution—the creation of man—to which Mark Twain lent his genius and which, in turn, gives universality to his humor and promises immortality to his fame.

In approaching the end of the pre-war period, we note that, in spite of his death, Mark Twain and his work still command the attention of German publishers and readers. Even though the interest of some of the former was more or less transitory, their activity, whether actuated by cultural or commercial motives, was nevertheless marked, and was noteworthy for the collective effort to strengthen and fortify his position in Germany. As for the publications themselves, these years furnish confirmation of the increasing popularity of the *Sketches, The Adventures of Tom Sawyer*, and *The Adventures of Huckleberry Finn*.

In the field of criticism, the early years of this period were fruitful in that they brought to the German public critical appraisals

---

[24] Halle a.S.: Niemeyer, 1897, I, 354.
[25] Elster classifies humor as humor of self-confidence, humor of sympathy. and socio-political humor.

of Mark Twain by two distinguished American scholars. These analyses are significant for their content; they are equally important because they lent further support to that body of German opinion which without minimizing the humorous phase of Mark Twain's activity, was advocating a wider and more serious approach. German readers might well have been impressed by a similarity in the approach of Smith and Henderson. Mark Twain's work, according to the former, is to be interpreted in the light of interesting contrasts, and his humor, which is the chosen means of illuminating those contrasts, is to be judged in the light of the social and political conditions in America. From the point of view of Henderson, Mark Twain emerges as a real moralist and philosopher with an intense interest in the deeper issues of life, and also as "America's greatest, most human sociologist in letters," a man with a marked "ability of social comprehension."

PART TWO

POST-WAR RECEPTION

V

REVIVAL OF INTEREST
1919-1925

Publications, 1919-1921——Steindorff——Bleibtreu——Publications, 1923-1925 ——German appraisal of *Mark Twain's Letters* and *Mark Twain's Autobiography*——Summary.

In the years immediately following the World War, the question of German book production becomes a matter of considerable moment. The book, always a foremost medium in the formation of German attitudes, was vitally affected by the political and economic upheaval. With the increase in the cost of living, there was also a corresponding increase in the cost of book production. Although the price of books did not increase proportionately to that of the commodities of daily life, production costs did. The business year 1919-1920 was most dismal and discouraging. Under financial conditions so unfavorable for the book market, it is a matter of especial interest that German publishers should have turned their attention to Mark Twain. In spite of disheartening conditions, tions, Velhagen & Klasing brought out a new school edition of *The Prince and the Pauper*,[1] Reclam three volumes of sketches,[2] and Hesse & Becker of Leipsic a volume each of *Tom Sawyers Abenteuer und Streiche* and *Huckleberry Finns Abenteuer und Fahrten*.[3]

Although the year 1921 did not show a pronounced improvement in economic stability, it nevertheless laid the foundation for a renewed and intensified interest in Mark Twain, which reached a high point in 1923. Within these three years, firms which had already been associated with the vogue of Mark Twain in Germany

---

[1] Series of English authors. CXXXV B.

[2] The one volume ("Reclam Universal-Bibliothek," No. 2072) was a reprint of the fourth of the six volumes of *Ausgewählte Skizzen,* which had appeared between 1878 and 1897. The other two volumes, *Die Geschichte der kapitolinischen Venus u. a. Skizzen* and *Der gestohlene weisse Elefant,* appeared as Volumes XXXIII and XXXIV of the "Reclams Automaten-Bücher" (1920). Both pamphlets were about twenty-eight pages in length and very reasonably priced.

[3] Incorporated into "Romane der Weltliteratur."

released further editions of works under their imprints;[4] the Insel-Verlag published the first (and until now the only) translation of *The Mysterious Stranger,* by Wilhelm Nobbe[5] under the title *Der geheimnisvolle Fremde. Eine Phantasie;* the Mitteldeutsche Verlagsanstalt Lehman & Fink a large volume[6] containing *Die Abenteuer Tom Sawyers und Huckleberry Finns (des Kameraden von Tom Sawyer);*[7] and the Stein-Verlag of Vienna the first and only translation of *A Connecticut Yankee at the Court of King Arthur* as *Ein Yankee am Hofe des Königs Artur.*[8] It can not be overlooked of course that the huge inflation in Germany in 1922 and 1923, reaching its crest in the early fall of the latter year, gave some impetus to the book market, as it did to the purchase of commodities and wares of every description. Nevertheless the expansion of publication of the American author's works in 1923 is impressive. That 1923 was a "Mark Twain year" in Germany must be attributed primarily to the persistent efforts of Ulrich Steindorff,[9] the son of the eminent Egyptologist of the University of Leipsic, Georg Steindorff, and those of his publisher, Ullstein of Berlin.

Steindorff frequently spent his college vacations with his grandmother in Berlin. It was on one of these "holidays" that she directed his attention to Mark Twain's sketches. Although he had read Walt Whitman, he had not known the works of the popular humorist. Ten years later, in 1912, the same year in which his

[4] Loewes of Stuttgart, for example, issued a fourth printing of *Prinz und Bettelknabe. Eine Erzählung für die reifere Jugend.*

[5] Nobbe had won considerable recognition with his translation, in 1905, of Henry D. Thoreau's *Walden.* Eugen Diederichs of Leipsic published it in that year under the title *Walden oder Leben in den Wäldern.*

[6] Vol. XII of "Meistererzähler der Weltliteratur."

[7] The translation is same as that published in 1900 and 1902 by Hendel of Halle a.S. It was prepared by H. Hellwag with an introduction by Dr. Franz Kwest.

[8] Vol. III (1923) of "Die phantastischen Bücher." The translation was furnished by J. Botstiber and J. Ott. The cover design and the pen etchings were contributed by the artist Danilowatz. Although this work appeared in the original in the Tauchnitz "Collection of British Authors" as early as 1890, almost thirty-three years elapsed before it was translated.

[9] Steindorff gained distinction as the author of *Panthea* (1911), a tragedy in five acts, and *Frau Cardinal* (1913), a comedy in three acts; and as translator of Kipling's *Plain Tales* (1912) and Kakuzo Okakuras' *Book of Tea* (1922). At present he is president of the "U. S. Library Association, Inc." at Westwood Village, Los Angeles, California.

first translation, Kipling's *Plain Tales,* appeared, he read *The Adventures of Tom Sawyer* in English. Then, for the first time, he understood why he as well as other German boys and girls had not become acquainted with Mark Twain's books. He found that the German translations of the author's works "missed many threads he had woven together, and that the original color of his humor had faded and the subtle design had been reversed into mere caricature." So intensely did Mark Twain appeal to him that there was no question in his mind but that the American humorist would in time replace the old-fashioned juvenile authors in the hearts of the boys and girls of post-war Germany. As early as 1918 Steindorff resolved to make "modernized" translations of *The Adventures of Tom Sawyer* and *The Adventures of Huckleberry Finn* that would be "mainly for the entertainment of boys and girls." In an essay in *The New York Times Book Review* of July 13, 1924, entitled "Mark Twain's Broad German Grin," Steindorff tells of the difficulties he encountered in convincing a German publisher of the feasibility of "reviving Mark Twain's works." He realized only too well that Mark Twain had never been exactly a "best seller," and that publishers would be a little wary about undertaking such a project in unfavorable economic times. Almost two years passed before he succeeded in persuading Ullstein, one of the most progressive and liberal publishing houses[10] in Germany, to take this enterprise in hand. During the summer of 1921 *Tom Sawyers Abenteuer* appeared. Several months before that, publication of this work was announced at the Spring Fair in Leipsic, where, as customarily, the booksellers of all Germany met and filed orders for Christmas. The agents were apparently so much interested in the unusual cover depicting in colors the scene where Tom Sawyer paints the fence that it soon became evident on the basis of the advanced Christmas orders that *"Tom Sawyers Abenteuer* would outstrip all its competitors in the market for juvenile books." Half a year later *The Adventures of Huckleberry Finn*[11] was issued. What was originally thought to be fare

---

[10] For years Ullstein published the oldest and best-known German liberal newspapers, the *Vossische Zeitung* and the *Berliner Morgenpost.*

[11] Albert Ludwig, in his review of this work in *Das literarische Echo* (XXIV, 943), commends Steindorff for his quite successful rendition of the dialect. Steindorff had given it "berlinische Färbung."

for juveniles was soon seen to appeal to adults. The popularity which the two books achieved was reflected in the demand for other works. At intervals of about six months, Ullstein then published Steindorff's translations[12] of *A Tramp Abroad* under the title *Bummel durch Europa*, *Roughing It* as *Durch Dick und Dünn*, and finally *Selections of Mark Twain's Sketches* as *Tolle Geschichten*.[13] All the books were printed on the cheapest of paper and bound in the cheapest cardboard so that they might be accessible to all.

It is highly possible, as Friedrich Schönemann, an accredited Mark Twain critic in Germany, points out,[14] that the "grotesquely exaggerated jackets" of the books tended to stress in the mind of the average German reader the "mad American humorist" rather than the "thinking artist." Assuming that the translator approved of the unusual designs, there is every reason to believe that he did not have such an objective in mind. Steindorff, it seems proper to presume, had a keen understanding of human nature. He knew that such a jacket, even though grotesque and exaggerated, would capture the imagination of German youth. That he himself did not think of Mark Twain as a humorist in the very narrow sense of the word is evident from the brief but animated discussion in his preface to the first volume. Here he endeavors to refute certain erroneous conceptions about Mark Twain. Taking cognizance of the fact that particularly in Germany Mark Twain was too widely regarded as a "joker," Steindorff pleads for an understanding of him as a humorist who, following the lesson of Shakespeare, was not a "joker" but "a philosopher smiling at the world around him and laughing with it . . . splitting the mist, coldly and mercilessly, but doing it by love." The true humorist, as he envisages him, is one who sees the world as it is, but whose wisdom is one of exaggeration. Mark Twain, he argues, saw the world in all its diversity; but "just as a microscope exaggerates and unfolds realities never seen before by the naked eye, so also do the microscopic eyes of Mark Twain enlarge and magnify the world in its 'most naked

---

[12] All of the following books carried unusual covers.

[13] This volume contained some fifteen sketches, notably the two literary hits: *Punch, Brother, Punch* and *The Speech on the Babies*.

[14] *Das literarische Echo*, XXV, 177, 1127; XXVI, 179.

nakedness,' with the result that the creations of his humor frequently appear to the average reader a thousand times more fantastic than the creations of any art . . . For under the microscope of humor reality is as variegated as the most variegated phantasy." In common with many German critics of the preceding years, Steindorff rejects the view which found expression in the American press, theater, and even in literature, that it is impossible for a foreigner to comprehend American humor.[15] He readily concedes that a foreigner may find it more difficult to understand American humor than a native American, but he explains this on the ground that American humor is directed first of all at America and that a translator can not assimilate or reproduce what is to him incomprehensible. But he categorically denies that humor has national boundaries; he rather holds to the theory that the American humor of a Mark Twain will become German humor when the translation into German conforms to, and harmonizes with, the original. Defending Mark Twain's artistic work as "world literature" and his Tom Sawyer as "as international as Shakespeare's Falstaff or Cervantes' Don Quixote," Steindorff pleads for an appreciation of Mark Twain as a creative mind that utilized humor as a means of expressing the truth as it conceived it. It is difficult to say just what part Steindorff played in the molding of opinion about Mark Twain in these years. In view of the circumstance, however, that the large Ullstein circulation offered him a favorable opportunity for reaching the rank and file of German readers, it is quite probable that his enthusiastic interpretation had considerable influence.

Very different in tone from Steindorff is the sharply critical but inadequate estimate by Karl Bleibtreu in his *Geschichte der englischen Literatur mit Einschluss der amerikanischen*.[16] Bleibtreu (1859-1928) was a very versatile writer,[17] active in all fields of literature, creative as well as critical. As an important exponent of consistent naturalism, he formulated the principles of the "Youngest Germany" movement in his *Revolution in der Literatur*

---

[15] Schönemann likewise dismisses this view as baseless. *Germanisch-Romanische Monatsschrift*, VIII (1920), 153.

[16] Bern: Bircher, 1923, pp. 205-209.

[17] Bleibtreu is most widely known as the author of the collection of naturalistic novelettes *Schlechte Gesellschaft*, of the novel *Grössenwahn*, and of the pamphlet *Revolution in der Literatur*.

(1885). From 1885 to 1890 he was one of the guiding hands of the *Magazin für die Literatur des In- und Auslandes* and the *Gesellschaft*. It was particularly in those years that he did some of his most striking work in the critical field. In the opinion of competent judges Bleibtreu was more important as a critic than as an original writer. Unusually bitter and brutally frank, he aroused constant antagonism and gradually lost influence in literary circles. At the time of the publication of the literary history mentioned above his prestige and influence had reached a low ebb. Nevertheless, the unfavorable picture which he draws of Mark Twain merits some consideration as one more illustration of the wide differences of opinion.

On the whole, there is little of interest to cite from the literary point of view. Bleibtreu repeats in substance the objections which other German critics had voiced. Like them, he minimizes Mark Twain's power of invention[18] and narrative skill.[19] He employs to some extent a familiar and generally effective type of ridicule to score him for his ignorance of finer culture and for his "typically American" tendency to talk about everything he does not understand. "An uncultured, superficial cad," "an arrogant, obstreperous prattler," "a rough rider of literature," "a kindred soul of Cook and Peary,"—these expressions characterize the tone of his criticism. On the other hand, he does give faint, grudging praise for vitality and power of observation to Mark Twain's descriptions of people, lands, and customs. He even approves of his objectives as a satirist and defender of the rights of the individual against society; but he strongly disapproves his methods. The technique of exaggeration which, as he concedes, Mark Twain employed successfully in a number of scenes in *Stormfield's Visit to Heaven* to symbolize the macrocosm, takes on the character, in the large bulk of his work, of "slaying the dead and murdering corpses." The humor of a Laurence Sterne and a Jean Paul, of a Raabe and a

---

[18] Bleibtreu's criticism on this point is directed mainly against the repeated use of the contrast between Tom and Huck, which, in his judgment, is merely Don Quixote and Sancho Panza translated into a modern setting.

[19] The *Celebrated Jumping Frog* he terms "a mere anecdotal sketch," and its popularity he describes as one of the "incomprehensibilities of the literary taste of the masses." Other stories, particularly the *$1,000,000 Banknote,* he finds so poorly told that "only a very immature mind could be amused."

Reuter he places far above that of a Mark Twain, while the wit of a Swift and a Byron far surpasses the American's laborious dealing with externalities. Bleibtreu's opinion of Mark Twain is summarized in his own conclusion: "It will remain significant for our time that a very serious social reformer full of youthful naïveté secured an audience through clownish tricks, as though the contemporary world were a circus, and gained the reputation of being the *greatest humorist* because he himself could not remain serious when his somersaults were accepted as the gallop of world humor. One would be equally justified in calling Carlyle a humorist, for his savage mockery makes better wit."

There is reason to believe that the public response to the Steindorff translations attracted the attention of other publishers. In 1924 C. Stephenson of Leipsic and Vienna issued a volume[20] containing thirty-seven selections from *The Innocents Abroad* as *Bummel durch das Mittelmeer; Die Kultur,* a German quarterly for science, literature, and art, carried in its June edition[21] nine sketches grouped under the title *Aus einem Wanderleben; Die Weltbühne*[22] published a translation of Mark Twain's *The War Prayer,* which he had dictated in 1904 or 1905 but which first appeared in 1923, entitled *Kriegsgebet;* and the so-called "Büchergilde Gutenberg," an organization established to promote the cultural interests of German printers, a volume of selections from Mark Twain's varied career under the title *Mit heiteren Augen. Geschichten.*[23] This edition was prefaced by an appropriate greeting and a very interesting résumé and estimate of the author's life and work by Ernst Preczang, an author and journalist, the editor of the Socialist periodical of fiction *In freien Stunden,* and a cofounder and active member of the "Gilde."[24]

The renewal of interest in Mark Twain's work was reflected particularly in the publications of the year 1925. Hesse & Becker

[20] Vol. VI of "Die lustigen Bücher."
[21] Pp. 1-33. These sketches, it was held, represented in particular the author's "humoristische Kleinmalerei."
[22] November, 1924, p. 758.
[23] These selections were taken from the six volume edition of Mark Twain's works published by Lutz of Stuttgart.
[24] Preczang's literary work included dramas (for example, *Gabrielle der Fischer,* 1911), novels (*Der Ausweg,* 1912), and poems (*Im Strom der Zeit,* 1908).

issued a reprint of *Mark Twains Werke. Auswahl in 3 Bänden*[25] and of *Tom Sawyers Abenteuer und Streiche* and *Huckleberry Finns Abenteuer und Fahrten;*[26] the Schillerbuchhandlung of Berlin also put out a volume[27] of *Tom Sawyers Abenteuer;* the Deutsche Buchgemeinschaft of Berlin, a volume[28] of *Die Streiche Tom Sawyers und Huckleberry Finns;* and M. Maschler of the same city, a volume[29] each of *Die Abenteuer Tom Sawyers* and *Die Abenteuer Huckleberry Finns.* Velhagen & Klasing added a new edition of the school text of *The Adventures of Tom Sawyer,*[30] and H. Opitz of Berlin a short pamphlet[31] of some thirty-two pages which contained a selection by Max Maria von Weber and Mark Twain's *Meine Uhr.*

More or less directly in the wake of the revival of interest in Mark Twain in the two years, 1924 and 1925, a number of articles appeared which are of some consequence to our study. The year 1924 brought only two,[32] and these were of an informative rather than critical character. That was also true of a number of studies in 1925. Two of these are, however, of some importance, since they point the way to a new orientation in the German attitude. Certain German students of American literature were impressed with the "new fashion of disapproval" which set in around 1920 in America. In that year the American critic, Van Wyck Brooks, in his *The Ordeal of Mark Twain,* advanced the theory that Mark

---

[25] First appearance in 1910.

[26] In the series "Romane der Weltliteratur."

[27] Vol. L of "Die bunten Romane der Weltliteratur."

[28] Vol. LXXIX. This edition was circulated only among the members of the Buchgemeinschaft.

[29] Each volume contained an introduction by Albert Erding.

[30] First appearance in 1914.

[31] Vol. II of the "Kurzschriftliche Übungshefte."

[32] In the one (*Alte und neue Welt,* LIX), Dr. A. Hüppy, a Swiss scholar, co-editor of the *Schweizerische Illustrierte Zeitung,* and a zealous advocate of English language instruction in Switzerland, re-examines *A Tramp Abroad* which, in his judgment, offers an adequate index to the literary powers of Mark Twain. He reviews the historical development of the work, and devotes considerable space to Mark Twain's temporary residence in Switzerland. The other article (*Der Tag, Unterhaltungsbeilage,* July 24, 1924) contains an interesting description of a visit by Mark Twain, in November of 1891, to Heinrich Seidel, the creator of *Leberecht Hühnchen.* Neither of these articles can be said to add anything of interest to the German criticism of Mark Twain as it has been examined up to this point.

Twain was "a creative force potentially great" but suppressed by "puritanical and materialistic elements in American life"; that this sense of frustration led to despair and bitterness; that he was a scorching critic of the social fabric, but that he betrayed his artistic integrity in order to conform to the respectability of the period. Although this "frustration theory" was aired in 1920, almost five years elapsed before it found public expression in Germany. Then Henry Lüdeke, professor at the school of Commerce at St. Gall, reviewed Brooks' work for the *Deutsche Literaturzeitung*.[33] Lüdeke limits himself in the main to a recapitulation of the facts which led Brooks to his conclusions. Although he does not agree with the American critic's deductions, he nevertheless considers the work a masterful presentation of a difficult problem. A similar analysis of the "spiritual tragedy" of Mark Twain, based unquestionably on Brooks' work, appeared in the *Frankfurter Zeitung* of August 12, 1925. It was a translation by Hermynia Zur Mühlen of Upton Sinclair's sharply critical analysis of Mark Twain's frustrated genius.

The attitude of the most responsible and best qualified critics indicates that this year must indeed be considered a landmark in Mark Twain criticism in Germany, for it marks the culmination of a series of contributions of exceptional importance by the foremost Mark Twain scholar in Germany, Friedrich Schönemann. Few foreign critics could be better qualified to write an intelligent appraisal of Mark Twain. After a brief service in other American institutions, Schönemann was for eight years, from 1913 to 1920, an instructor in Harvard University. His travels and daily contacts with the rank and file of Americans, even though at a time when American-German relations were not the most cordial, enabled him to study America at close range and to equip himself thoroughly for his future task as political and literary interpreter. As early as 1920 the *Germanisch-Romanische Monatsschrift*[34] published a discussion of American humor, in which he sought to trace Mark Twain's rôle in its development. The following year he turned his attention to an analysis of Mark Twain's *Welt-*

---

[33] N.F. 2, 1925.
[34] VIII (1920), 152-164; 216-227.

anschauung, which appeared then in *Englische Studien*,[35] and followed it in the same journal in 1922 with a review of the Mark Twain literature that had appeared in America between 1910 and 1920. In 1923 the *Archiv für das Studium der neueren Sprachen und Literatur*[36] published his rather lengthy discussion of *Mark Twain's Letters*.[37] Two years later, 1925, Schönemann commented on *Mark Twain's Autobiography*[38] and also issued his most important study of the American writer, *Mark Twain als literarische Persönlichkeit*.[39] This monograph, together with the early articles, constitutes the most extensive analysis of Mark Twain's literary art in Germany and is therefore deserving of consideration in a separate chapter. For the present we shall confine ourselves to an examination of Schönemann's criticism of the posthumous *Mark Twain's Letters* and *Mark Twain's Autobiography*.

Mark Twain's Letters appeared in 1917. In America, critics were by no means in agreement as to their unique value. Those who expected unforeseen disclosures or "food for vulgar curiosity" were doomed to disappointment; those, however, who sought in the letters a naïve expression of his individuality, attached considerable import to their publication, even though they did not call it a "literary event." In Germany, the publication of the letters did not attract much attention. In fact, practically six years elapsed before the book was honored with a review by Schönemann, at that time professor of *Amerikakunde* in the university at Münster in Westphalia.

At the very outset, Schönemann criticizes the form in which the letters appeared. They were arranged in two volumes, with editorial comment by Albert Bigelow Paine, the official biographer and custodian of the Mark Twain letters and papers. Schönemann does not underestimate Paine's contribution, but he does take exception to the eulogistic tone of the editorial annotations. He is, moreover, irritated by the practice of the literary executor in

---

[35] LV, 53-84.
[36] CXLIV, 184-213.
[37] Arranged, with editorial comment, by Albert Bigelow Paine. Two volumes. Harper and Brothers Publ. New York, 1917.
[38] *Hannoverscher Kurier*, Aug. 5, 1925; *Magdeburger Zeitung*, Oct. 4, 1925.
[39] *Jenaer Germanistische Forschungen*, VIII (Jena: Verlag der Frommannschen Buchhandlung, 1925).

withholding certain material from publication.[40] In his judgment the treatment of a literary legacy should be left solely and alone to the tact and integrity of the critic. The universal import of these intimate letters, however, which were written under the stress of circumstances and with no thought of publication, he holds lies primarily in their value as documentary evidence of the private and personal life, not of the author Mark Twain, but of the man Mr. Clemens.[41] With their prodigious scope and variety in content, these letters mirror the fertility and flexibility of Mr. Clemens' mind and document some of the dominant characteristics in the development of American life. In his discussion of this particular phase, Schönemann calls attention to the fact that the Civil War and its resulting tasks and problems exerted a very disturbing influence on the life of the country and that young Clemens did not escape the forces of the time. A number of personal characteristics[42] are examined at some length to show, by way of clarification, that Clemens was in reality a product of the conditions of the time. Yet our critic does not find anywhere in the letters even an intimation of the struggles of the Civil War which transformed the national life.[43] It is, therefore, not only what Clemens revealed in the letters that may form a basis for understanding him; the omissions, he contends, are equally valuable in throwing light upon his character.

As might be expected in the case of an author with such a tremendously wide acquaintance, the character of the recipients of his letters was extremely varied. Schönemann is primarily interested in those addressed to Howells, the arbiter of literary taste in the United States at that time, and to Mrs. Clemens. Those to Howells extended over a period of some forty years and

---

[40] Paine commented that the letters were "reasonably complete."

[41] This explains the title of Schönemann's article, "Mr. Samuel Langhorne Clemens."

[42] Schönemann enumerates particularly "a native rashness and impetuosity," "an exaggerated spirit of self-reliance" or "Anglo-Saxon individualism," and finally "a strongly adventurous spirit," which, together with a baseless optimism and an exuberant imagination, led him on to unheard of speculations and frequently impossible undertakings, culminating in a sort of personal bankruptcy. These characteristics, he feels, reflect the contemporary spirit of unrest and haste.

[43] Schönemann also finds very little information in the letters regarding purely literary aspects.

are therefore of inestimable value in reaching a proper understanding of the relationship between the two men. On the other
hand, the very small number of letters to Mrs. Clemens has sur-
prised the average European reader who always was given to
understand that Clemens enjoyed an unusually happy married life
and that, judged by American standards, his wife was a cultured
woman. But one must not forget, Schönemann points out, that
Mrs. Clemens usually accompanied her husband on his various
trips, that opportunities for writing were naturally less numerous,
that Mr. Clemens was characteristically Anglo-Saxon in his utter
reserve in the expression of his emotions, and that this reserve was
strengthened by his wife's native "New England nature."

Measured by European standards, these letters, in our critic's
judgment, show certain deficiencies. Even though they contain
disclosures which discretion forbade including in his published
works, they are lacking in revelations such as are characteristic
of European and particularly of German private correspondence.
Self-introspection, he says, is not a distinguishing mark of the
American, who very rarely becomes a victim of his own experiences, because he never reveals himself completely in his association with others; consequently, his letters do not disclose a serious
exploration of the soul or a profound experience of the world. The
letters also lack the elegant epistolary skill of the French and,
because of the author's known indifference to women, a certain
charm of social companionship. Clemens' experience as a journalist, Schönemann emphasizes, trained him to jot down very com-
pactly moral and political "discharges of his soul," and reflects
itself in a very vigorous manner of expression, particularly noticeable in the letters of condemnation.

From the German point of view, the publication of *Mark
Twain's Autobiography* in 1925 also made a step in the direction
of a clearer understanding of the man and his work. For years
the readers of Mark Twain throughout the world were led to look
forward with keen anticipation to the publication of this work.
Mark Twain had frequently expressed the intention of witholding
it, till after his death. "Speaking from the grave, rather than with
my living tongue," he felt that he could be as "frank and free and

unembarrassed as a love letter." This solemn prefatory promise, coupled with his definition[44] of what an autobiography should be, and the confident assurance with which he undertook this work,[45] aroused an interest which was intensified by the publication of his letters and the Paine biography. The public naturally looked for revelations of the author's self and about the endless procession of his acquaintances and friends, for a searching accounting of his outer and inner life. With the publication of the two volumes in 1925, German as well as American critics gave expression to their disillusionment. They found nothing new, nothing refreshingly original, nothing of intrinsic value for a deeper insight into the philosophy and the literary environment of Mark Twain. What they did find was a substantiation of their fears that thoughtful consideration for friends and neighbors, for the traditions and sensibilities of the American nation, would keep his confidences well within conventional limits and form a more or less unconscious barrier to a completely reliable commentary. Thus the autobiography lacked, as Schönemann[46] puts it, "the preliminary condition of a frank and truthful self-revelation." "A rambling complex," "shapeless," "no continuity or chronological sequence," "ruminative,"—these are some of the characterizations of the work.

Yet irrespective of these deficiencies, our German commentators direct attention to some redeeming features of the autobiography. Sil-Vara,[47] a correspondent for German and Austrian papers prior to the outbreak of the World War, for example, considers it sufficiently interesting to devote an article to a résumé of the contents, stressing incidents and anecdotes that help to illuminate the author's youthfulness, humor, and humanity. Schönemann, on the other hand, approaches the autobiography from a more analytical and utilitarian point of view. He is predominantly concerned with its intrinsic value to the critic. Much of the material he finds delightfully charming and refreshing. The chapters deal-

---

[44] Mark Twain's theory of a successful autobiography, as evidenced in his own work, was "to roam up and down the years without any attempt at sequence of event or deadly accuracy of detail or date." Cf. Mark Twain's letter, dated March 14, 1904, to Howells.

[45] *Magdeburger Zeitung*, October 4, 1925.

[46] *Ibid.*

[47] *Neue Freie Presse*, August 13, 1925.

ing with Mark Twain's experiences in Nevada, his acquaintance with Theodore Roosevelt and Grover Cleveland, and the political chapters, in which his cutting satire predominates,—these, he admits, are all informative and instructive for the critic. Of historical significance he finds only Mark Twain's remarks about Grant and the latter's account of his relations with the Century Company. Considered as a whole, the autobiography is commended as an important source of biographical information, a most vivid and entrancing diary, each line of which is said to bear the imprint of the author's bold and original personality. The very fact that Mark Twain's method was methodless, that he suddenly grasped a subject, discussed it as long as it interested him, and then with equal rapidity dropped it when it had lost its appeal, makes the work absorbingly readable. The reaction of the fascinated reader, Schönemann predicts, will be one of enjoyment and complete relaxation.

In summarizing Mark Twain's reception in Germany in the decade just discussed, it becomes apparent that his popularity, which had begun to wane temporarily in some respects during the years of the World War, was stimulated primarily by the concentrated efforts of one of his staunchest supporters, Ulrich Steindorff, and of his publisher, Ullstein of Berlin. It may be said, in fact, that Steindorff's service lay not so much in reviving, in general, a Mark Twain interest in Germany as in reclaiming Mark Twain for German youth.

Though rather belatedly, German criticism in these years takes note of the posthumous works of the American author and recognizes their publication as a more hopeful step towards clarification. There is substantial evidence also of the conflicting appraisals of Mark Twain and his art which had characterized German criticism from the very beginning. This decade, however, is dominated by the emergence of the most important Mark Twain critic in Germany and with it by a notable progress in the serious interpretation of Mark Twain as a literary personality.

VI

SCHÖNEMANN'S APPRAISAL OF MARK TWAIN'S
LITERARY PERSONALITY, 1925

Mark Twain in the field of criticism——The American humorist——The un-
literary Mark Twain——The anti-romanticist——The philosopher of history
——The essayist——The narrator——Critical exposition of Mark Twain's
Weltanschauung——Summary.

In his work *Mark Twain als literarische Persönlichkeit*,[1] Schönemann confines himself to an investigation of what he calls Mark
Twain's "style." Interpreting "style" in the very broadest sense,
he analyzes the various phases which, in his estimation, comprise
a literary personality. Critics in general,[2] he contends, have not
fully grasped Mark Twain as a literary personality and consequently have never thoroughly examined his style. There was
always a tendency, he finds, to stress individual phases and to
neglect the author's whole personality as the human and spiritual
basis of his activity.

In his discussion of the more recent American interpretations
of Mark Twain,[3] Schönemann turns his attention primarily to a
criticism of Van Wyck Brooks' *The Ordeal of Mark Twain*.[4]
Brooks, as has been pointed out,[5] advanced the thesis that Mark
Twain was a great genius, a real artist who should have attained
greatness but was frustrated by the period in which he lived. In
general, Schöneman rejects Brooks' interpretation on the ground
that it judges not an individual American but the America which
produced him, that in the conflict with the America of yesterday

---

[1] *Jenaer Germanistische Forschungen*, No. 8. Jena: Verlag der Frommannschen
Buchhandlung, 1925. Schönemann's work was honored with a number of reviews
by German educators. In the course of the following discussion, we shall supplement Schönemann's analysis with the critical reactions of these reviewers.

[2] In this connection Schönemann draws briefly from authentic sources of information and reviews the critical reception of Mark Twain in England, France, Germany, and America. This forms the main substance of the first chapter, entitled
"Mark Twain in der Kritik," which may also be considered a preface to the
work.

[3] Schönemann gives a very brief résumé of the appreciations by Henderson and
Fred Lewis Pattee.

[4] New York, 1920.

[5] See Chapter Five.

it does not do full justice to Mark Twain, who was a part of that America and who, in fact, was the first to give literary expression to that epoch. Brooks, Schönemann contends, cannot fully comprehend Mark Twain because he underestimates and dislikes the America of Mark Twain's day.

Interesting in this connection is also the reaction of the Swiss critic Lüdeke.[6] Although he does not accept wholeheartedly the explanations and conclusions of the American critic, he nevertheless does not reject this new picture as something beyond the realm of possibility. Brooks' work, in his opinion, is merely one expression of a post-war tendency. The war, Lüdeke explains, released forces which severely criticized the old America and desired to build up a new ideal. In literature this movement led to a "revaluation of existing greatness," and Mark Twain, the symbol of the former America, became one of the first affected by this. Lüdeke agrees with Brooks in so far as human fate is subject to, and determined by, one's native character and environment. He is also willing to accept the thesis that the "unpropitiousness of circumstances" and the weakness in Mark Twain's own character were dominant factors in the shaping of his career. But he is not so sure that Mark Twain would have developed essentially otherwise under other more favorable conditions. He points to Lincoln and Walt Whitman, to whom Mark Twain was not attracted, as definite proof that strong natures can rise above the conditions of the time. What Mark Twain lacked was the courage and the will that was characteristic of them as well as of a Tolstoy and a Dostoyefsky. One cannot ignore this fundamental defect, Lüdeke argues, and yet accept "an absolute capacity of the soul for development" as Brooks does.

Schönemann seems to stand alone in interpreting Brooks' work as an attempt to explain Mark Twain in the light of Freudian psychology, or of "a naïve and uncritical American imitation of the Viennese writer."[7] Those German scholars, with one notable exception, who undertook a review of Schönemann's *Mark Twain als literarische Persönlichkeit*, either failed to detect this analysis

---

[6] *Deutsche Literaturzeitung*, XLVI (Sept. 12, 1925), 1802-1807.
[7] *Op. cit.*, p. 10.

and consequently did not comment on it, or, having noticed it, advisedly disregarded it or tacitly accepted it. To interpret Mark Twain's work in the light of Freudian psychology, Lüdeke explains, would give a false picture of his work. There is absolutely no question, in his mind, of a disturbing sexuality, of dream interpretations, or of the "confusion of artist and work." Lüdeke's argument is that Brooks painfully avoided a psycho-analytical interpretation.[8]

After a general criticism of Brooks' book, Schönemann turns to the principal task in hand, the analysis of Mark Twain's style. To this end, he treats Mark Twain first of all as "the American humorist," and seeks to trace and to define the forces that directed his development as a humorist.[9] Starting out with the fixed idea that, regardless of the occupation Mark Twain followed, he was always by profession an author and a creative force, Schönemann contends that he was forced into the calling of humorist by circumstances which he did not understand and over which he had no control. The Civil War, it is pointed out, put an end to his career as a respected and admired pilot on the Mississippi, and encouraged the journey to Nevada. In contrast to Paine, Mark Twain's official biographer, and Lüdeke,[10] who are inclined to explain this journey as an attempt to evade the war, Schönemann accepts Brooks' view that it was a trip for enjoyment, but he rejects the latter's contention that it was also a moral danger for the budding author. In common with certain American critics, he also stresses the tremendous influence of the boisterous life of the pioneer in the Wild West, with its strange contrasts and contradictions. Mark Twain, he points out, had the choice of being one of such a community, or of being different, "offensively conspicuous and a subject of remark." But the fact that he became one of them and that he caused people to laugh at their own conspicuous eccentricities does not justify, in the opinion of Schönemann, the conclusion drawn by Brooks that the West finally made him a pioneer in the worst sense. Clemens, our critic holds, did not surrender himself completely to his milieu. What is remarkable, says

[8] *DL,* XLVI, 1808 f.
[9] *Op. cit.,* pp. 12-30.
[10] *DL,* XLVI, 1808.

Schönemann, is that Mark Twain was himself and remained himself in spite of all destructive forces.

In its struggle for existence, the West created a specialized brand of humor, and this so-called "Western humor" became for Mark Twain a means of self-defense, a deliverance, a safety-valve for self-control, which found its first literary expression in the newspaper. Here again, Schönemann takes issue on the one hand with those critics[11] who contend that Mark Twain created nothing of literary value in this early period, and on the other with those who insist that he experimented until (for practical reasons) he came to humor. In his judgment, these early literary products should not be considered as merely vigorous, miscellaneous "journalism," but as an excellent apprenticeship for the budding author[12] and useful training in the development of his descriptive prose. Mark Twain would never have become "the master of descriptive prose" without that training in journalism. In contrast with Brooks, who was inclined to praise his satire but to question his humor, Schönemann lays stress on the fact that humor and satire go hand in hand. Satire, he argues, is only a part of the whole and is always present as "the intellectual meaning of humor."

Our critic also subscribes to the view, which has abundant critical support in Germany, that a certain pessimism was from the very beginning an integral element of his humor. The fundamental basis for this pessimism he finds in Mark Twain's keen observation of man and his bitter personal experiences; and to those early impressions of life and mankind, increased proportionately to the penetration by each new experience, he attributes the wild and deliberate effectiveness of his humor. A consideration of Mark Twain's conception and treatment of human beings leads Schönemann to draw an interesting comparison with Benjamin Franklin. Both inherited a certain distrust of mankind; but while Franklin took practical advantage of his fellowmen, Clemens, "with his artistic phantasy and great heart, wavered between love and contempt." Whereas Brooks frequently speaks of Mark Twain's dual personality" and his "combination of barbaric force

[11] For example, Brooks and Paine.
[12] Steindorff also takes the view that Mark Twain was not a journalist, even though he wrote many hundred articles for the newspapers.

and intense sweetness," Schönemann stresses rather the strong dualism of reason and feeling which explains on the one hand the satirist, and on the other "the friend of mankind." Whether the one or the other predominated, he says, depended upon his moods and circumstances. Mark Twain, he points out, was a highly sensitive nature. Being of a fiery temperament, he usually acted first and then reflected. Neither Schönemann nor Lüdeke agrees with Brooks when the latter terms this tendency "a perfect definition of immaturity." But Lüdeke agrees with Brooks' contention that Mark Twain never reached a practical adjustment or synthesis of heart and reason.[13] Schönemann rejects Paine's view[14] that Mark Twain had had only "pessimistic intervals" and was never really a pessimist.

The charge that Mark Twain was merely a "funny man" is likewise analyzed at some length. Schönemann ascribes this view of him to various causes: jealousy on the part of other writers and Mark Twain's spirited self-defense, the imaginative appeal of his personal appearance, and his persistent *Narrentum*. The danger of such a conception lies in its tendency to degrade the author by subjective standards of readers and listeners, a danger which was increased because Mark Twain did not always resist the temptation to court the approval of the masses by means of the commonplace. Thus critics frequently cite his letter to Andrew Lang[15] in support of their argument that the former sought the approval of the masses[16] and consequently was merely a "funny man." Schönemann challenges their conclusion and counters with the assertion that even if the mere amusement of the masses formed one phase of his work, it was certainly supplemented by other, more human and artistic values.

Schönemann then takes up the charge, made by readers and supported by numerous critics,[17] that Mark Twain was in the

---

[13] *DL*, XLVI, 1808.

[14] *Mark Twain's Letters*, p. 767.

[15] *Ibid.*, p. 527.

[16] Brooks stressed not only Mark Twain's "love of applause," but also his vanity. This trait in his character forms actually, in Lüdeke's judgment, the basis of Brooks' entire analysis. Schönemann is inclined to attribute it to the American desire for great national characters, to the author's "self-instruction," and *Narrentum*. Cf. *DL*, XLVI, 1808.

[17] For example, a critic in the *Bookman*, XXXI, 366; also Howells.

highest degree "unliterary."[18] This, he finds, overlooks the influence of his years as a printer's apprentice and journeyman printer. These years must have awakened not only a stimulus for reading, as was the case with Benjamin Franklin, Walt Whitman, and Howells, but also a discriminating sense for good and bad literature. Perhaps they laid the foundation for the achievement of a style. Mark Twain, moreover, was too gifted not to have known what was valuable in literature, in spite of all personal hindrances. However, our critic finds it hard to present conclusive evidence of this. Mark Twain, he concedes, frequently confessed that he was self-taught, and more than once left the impression that he lacked a discriminating literary appreciation. Nevertheless, Schönemann does undertake a defense of Mark Twain as a "literary" character, based on a careful analysis of the author's reading. The large number of titles and references in his books and letters, and the citations scattered throughout his works are held to give ample proof of extensive reading. The intellectual exchange between England and America (with the American press as the principal medium), the critical material in periodicals, the Browning cult and later the "Meredith epidemic" exercised an unmistakable influence upon the writers of the period from which Mark Twain could not have been immune. Among the works in English literature which might have had a positive influence are the Bible, Bunyan's *Pilgrim's Progress*, Boswell's *Life of Johnson*, English novels, autobiographies, and essays. In addition one should not overlook the frequent visits which enabled him to make the acquaintance of important English personalities.

The influence of Shakespeare is not exactly convincingly demonstrated. Schönemann simply takes it for granted that he read and knew him.[19] Alois Brandl,[20] a recognized Shakespeare authority, a frequent contributor to scholarly periodicals, and a co-editor of the *Archiv für das Studium der neueren Sprachen und Literaturen*, is inclined to the view that Mark Twain may have intentionally disregarded Shakespeare. Shakespeare, he says, raises the weaknesses of man to colossal dimensions, while Mark Twain

[18] Schönemann, *op. cit.*, pp. 31-50.
[19] *Ibid.*, p. 41.
[20] *Die Literatur*, XXVII, 628.

proceeds negatively and reduces the great and the pathetic. On the other hand, Walther Fischer,[21] a professor at the Technical Institute in Dresden and likewise widely known for his studies in American literature, seeks an explanation of Mark Twain's indifference to Shakespeare in his strange essay *Is Shakespeare Dead?*. In this essay, in which the pro-Bacon proof culminates in the "lawyer argument," he disposes of the historical conception of Shakespeare's person as a "superstition," just as he considers everything that is not American and republican, "superstition." However, not one of the German critics presents any evidence to show that Mark Twain particularly valued Shakespeare.

On the other hand, Schöneman feels that the English humorists may have exerted an influence, though it is difficult to define it. There is a literary tradition in humor, as Thackeray pointed out, and Mark Twain, our critic contends, could not escape it any more than any other humorist; but he could break through tradition more easily because his humorous talent and general artistic ability were so original and powerful. In addition, he had a new field of activity—America, particularly the West.

Even though Mark Twain was influenced by Charles Lamb's essays, our critic does not feel that he was a humorist of the Lamb school. He is more inclined to emphasize his relationship with Swift. Mark Twain, he says, was a satirist of Swift's spirit, particularly "in his intellectual and humorous attitude toward the world." His philosophy, with its mechanistic interpretation of man, reminds him strongly of Swift; but while Swift remained rigidly consistent, Mark Twain permitted himself mental reservations and compromises. Like Swift, he also wrote works for the "universal improvement of mankind." He was opposed to the religious sects, and like Swift, he saw in human nature an element of madness. Nevertheless, he was not willing to follow Swift into the depths of the latter's hatred of the human race.

The relation to Dickens is stressed at some length.[22] The American critic Stuart Sherman[23] had contended that Mark Twain revealed in the *Gilded Age* "a certain flavor of Dickens." Schöne-

---

[21] *Englische Studien*, LXI, 139.
[22] Schönemann, *op. cit.*, pp. 44-48.
[23] *Cambridge History*, III, 6, 14.

mann rejects this view on the ground that most of the characters were drawn from life itself. Yet he does admit the existence of a striking similarity between the petty bourgeois milieu of the *Gilded Age* and the many tradesmen of Dickens' world. Likewise he calls attention to a marked resemblance in the characters of Colonel Sellers and Mr. Micawber; but the inner relationship between these two he attributes to their common descent from Don Quixote. It is primarily in their conception and presentation of children, Schönemann points out, that these two authors deviate. Dickens paints the child with the eyes of an adult. Mark Twain, on the other hand, portrays his children, for example Tom and Huck, never as heroes for adults, but always as heroes in their own sphere. Sentimental traits exist, but our critic justifies them on the ground that sentimentality belongs to youth.[24] Dickens' portrayal of David Copperfield depicts a life from youth to manhood; Mark Twain, in contrast, is interested only in presenting a section of life, supplemented, however, by the entire civilization which surrounded his own youth.[25] In Dickens almost all the children appear in connection with some calling; in Mark Twain the boy's life is freedom and whitewashing. These similarities and dissimilarities may suggest an influence of Dickens. Mark Twain, Schönemann submits, may have learned from Dickens in the manner of character delineation; but in the psychological presentation of child life, the American author certainly surpassed Dickens.

American literature, in our critic's estimation, also contributed its share to the literary education of Mark Twain. His own instinct, the current convention, and perhaps the judgment of periodicals determined his reading. His personal relations with contemporary American authors who were influenced by the same waves of literary taste must have been an important factor in stimulating interest in contemporary works. In contrast with the

[24] Schönemann finds it extraordinary that Mark Twain avoided the most sentimental trait of American literature, namely mother love. *Op. cit.*, p. 47.

[25] This is true particularly in *The Adventures of Tom Sawyer* and *The Adventures of Huckleberry Finn*. But the life presented in the latter work, Schönemann feels, has not the original and immediate effect of that in the former in which the fate of Huck and his struggle against civilization is more striking and impressive. Schönemann seems to favor *The Adventures of Tom Sawyer*, whereas American criticism is inclined to prefer the other. *Op. cit.*, pp. 47 f.

early German critics, Schönemann is inclined to minimize the importance of the relationship between Mark Twain and Bret Harte. On the basis of the letters he finds it no longer possible to put them together, as one associates, for example, in German literature Keller and Meyer or Liliencron and Dehmel.[26] Such a juxtaposition he considers dangerous because "it unites in thought and time what had no real unity of life and production." Although they resemble each other strikingly in their beginnings and in their selection of material and its treatment, they nevertheless differ in character, career, and creative procedure. On the other hand, he assigns greater importance to the help Mark Twain received from William Dean Howells. Howells was the authoritative editor of the most important monthly magazine in the United States and consequently was in a position to exercise great influence as an arbiter of literary taste. For years Mark Twain submitted his manuscripts to him and Howells assisted him in the elimination of such "inelegancies and coarsenesses" as Mrs. Clemens had overlooked. It is to Howells as a critic of form that Mark Twain is to some extent indebted. From the German point of view, the importance of a parallel between Howells and Mark Twain is said to lie in the fact that they represent two specific directions of literary Americanism.[27] Both are genuinely American, yet the one is "virile, independent, awkward, rugged, coarse," the other "well-bred, polite, dexterous, cautiously reserved, and therefore seldom really independent and vigorous." They represent two sides of the American being which, combined, may give us a picture of the "American soul."

To complete the analysis of Mark Twain's extensive reading, our critic calls attention briefly to the educational contribution of the translations of ancient classical works and of modern world literature, and to the formative influence of numerous French and German books, as well as works of a biographical, religious, and metaphysical character.

Closely allied with the charge that Mark Twain was "unliterary" is the claim that he was "anti-romantic." This mistaken con-

---

[26] *Archiv*, CXLIV, 209.
[27] Cf. *Englische Studien*, LV, 83.

ception our critic ascribes to the strange contrast between his spontaneous approval of Cervantes and his thorough-going repudiation
of Scott as a literary model. Taking up the question of the "influence of Cervantes," Schönemann recognizes a definite reflection
of Cervantes' procedure in certain works.[28] In *Innocents Abroad*
it is found in the genuine artistic phantasy of the author; in *The
Adventures of Huckleberry Finn* in the transformation of the
prototype of Huck so as to present a foil to Tom;[29] and in *A Connecticut Yankee* in the conscious satire on knighthood and its
romanticism. Satire was a part of Mark Twain's native endow-
ment; consequently, Schönemann declares, Cervantes could only
stimulate it and confirm him in his tendency to destroy the obsolete, the "outmoded, the devitalizing in history" by means of
laughter. Schönemann does not go so far as to maintain that the
humorist Cervantes made the humorist Mark Twain, but he does
contend that Mark Twain's deepest conception of humor is in-
conceivable without the Spanish model. Both, he finds, to a great
extent base their humor on the same contrast, the contrast between imaginative and unimaginative characters; similarly, both
utilize the specific humor which rests upon linguistic misunder-
standing, even though it may be merely an accidental coincidence.
But in the use of slang the American author sets his own original
standard.

The very forces which impelled Mark Twain to an interest in
Cervantes are also cited to explain his sharp rejection of Scott.
Schönemann acknowledges a limited influence of Scott in the
South, but he rejects Mark Twain's contention that the "Sir
Walter disease" was so formidable there. The fact that he (Mark
Twain) exaggerated not only the Scott contagion in the South
but also *Don Quixote's* influence on the North and South is in-
terpreted rather as a reflection of an American tendency toward
"general statements." What Schönemann finds particularly per-

---

[28] *Op. cit.*, pp. 51-54. In his discussion of the influence of *Don Quixote* on Mark
Twain, Schönemann leans heavily on Olin Harris Moore's article "Mark Twain and
Don Quixote" (*Publications of the Modern Language Association*, XXXVII, 324-
346).

[29] Schönemann also thinks he has found a "direct borrowing." The phantastic attack of Tom's gang on the Sunday School picnic, he says, is strongly reminiscent
of the famous attack on the herd of sheep in Cervantes. *Op. cit.*, p. 52.

plexing is Mark Twain's indifference to the youthfulness and vitality of Scott's art. That he saw in Scott only the feudal author, the snob, and disregarded his humor leads our critic to ask: "Why, then, did Mark Twain reject Scott?" The answer he seeks in the conflict within Mark Twain himself, in the conflict between his romantic and anti-romantic tendencies.[30]

At this juncture various propensities are cited which permit a fairly accurate estimate of Mark Twain's romantic nature. Mark Twain, it is held, was by nature romantically inclined. Schöne-mann, as well as Walther Fischer,[31] regards the intense and vehe-ment pursuit of phantoms in such figures as Tom and Colonel Sellers as the literary expression of a recognized family trait. Even Satan in *The Mysterious Stranger* he would term a roman-ticist, but a romanticist according to the German conception of romantic irony, for he destroys by means of reason what he has constructed by his emotions. In fact, the entire conception of *The Mysterious Stranger* suggests a romantic approach, as does its philosophy, that life is only a vision, a dream, a thought—a form of romantic solipsism.[32] Mark Twain's bitter dislike of many modern realistic novels, with their "fidelity to sordid and ugly conditions," our critic is inclined to attribute not so much to "his puritanical narrowness, moral prudery, or Anglo-Saxon reticence," as to "the instinctive antipathy of a romantic soul to the mirroring of un-pleasant reality." Mark Twain, to be sure, presented life as he had seen and experienced it, but a life in which poetry and truth are inseparable. Even where he reproduced life in the style of a reporter, the content was embellished or at least *enthässlicht* by his style.

A predilection for dreams, Schönemann continues, points to a romantically inclined nature. Mark Twain repeatedly gave evi-dence of an intense interest in all peculiarities of the human soul. He had no understanding for "hymns to the night," but he was superstitious, and his interest in the shadow side of consciousness,

[30] *Op. cit.*, pp. 61-72.

[31] *Englische Studien*, LXI, 137.

[32] Walther Fischer, on the other hand, argues that the particular view (that man is but a thought) goes back to the psychology of William James, who established that "the I ... is a thought, at each moment different from that of the last moment." *Ibid.*, pp. 137 f.

in occult and psychic phenomena, never waned. Romantic is also "the inclination to wrap oneself in the garment of distant ages or distant lands."[33] Schönemann, however, does not fail to point out that even though the impulse to the story may be romantic, its conception and execution are realistic. Mark Twain's enthusiasm for nature is also interpreted as the expression of a genuinely romantic passion. Schönemann is of the opinion that he did cultivate a sense for nature, even though he gave very little literary evidence of his reaction to nature. This strange paradox may be the result of his predilection for "large scenery"[34] or of his Anglo-Saxon artistic temperament as a whole. However, in the last analysis, our critic seems to think that Mark Twain's romanticism had definite limits which must be sought in the author's innermost being.

Finally, Mark Twain's love of music is interpreted as the reflection of a romantic inclination. But, as Schönemann points out, the difficulty in judging his attitude toward music lies in the nature of his approach. A humorous attitude toward art, beauty, or even music implies not so much a danger in the employment of humor as a danger that the humorist may transcend the bounds of propriety and leave an indelicate and coarse impression. Brooks characterized this tendency "to degrade beauty and debase distinction" as "the general tendency of Mark Twain's humor"; Schönbach[35] had ascribed it to a lack of cultural refinement. Schönemann would rather seek the explanation in Mark Twain's Americanism. Even though we may agree with the German critic Lüdeke[36] that a mere love for music by no means identifies the romanticist, we are inclined to agree with Schönemann's inference that anyone appreciative of Händel, Schubert, Chopin, and Beethoven is not entirely lost to music or to romanticism.

Although conflicting forces within led Mark Twain to a whole-hearted acceptance and conscious imitation of Don Quixote, the ultimate reason for his rejection of Scott Schönemann would find

---

[33] The definition is Oscar Walzel's. Cf. his *Vom Geistesleben alter und neuer Zeit*, Leipsic: Insel-Verlag, 1922, p. 108.

[34] This view was advanced by Carl Van Doren in *The American Novel*, New York: The Macmillan Co., 1922, p. 186.

[35] *Gesammelte Aufsätze*, p. 373.

[36] *DL*, XLVI, N.F. 2, 1810.

in his conception of history. His knowledge of history, his political views, and his picture of the world and of humanity were directly opposed to the sentimentalized history of a Scott. Scott's world was a falsification of historical life which Mark Twain strenuously opposed. In his discussion of Mark Twain as a "philosopher of history," Schönemann confines himself to an analysis of the possible influence of individual historians. Among the more important he mentions Suetonius for his vivid account of the cruelty and immorality of the Roman Empire; Goldsmith's *Citizen of the World* (described by Clemens as "a *beau idéal* of fine writing") for a thoroughly pessimistic estimate of all European history;[37] Lecky's *History of European Morals;* and the *Diary of Samuel Pepys*. Pepys' strong appeal he ascribes to an identity of common interests. Both were of humble origin; both advanced through their own strenuous efforts to positions of greater recognition; both had common intellectual interests. In Pepys Mark Twain recognized a friend of books, a lover of music, and a humorist with a taste for "tall tales" and a picaresque sense for knavish traits. From Pepys he received many vivid impressions of English life in the reigns of Charles II and James II. The picture of England of that day, with its political corruption, immorality, and lack of national dignity, must have emphasized and strengthened his historical conception of the madness of monarchy and feudalism, and the necessity of republicanism. From our critic's point of view, Mark Twain's glorification of a republic at any cost is uncritical and indiscriminate, reflecting above all an American characteristic.

Of far greater significance is Schönemann's detailed analysis of Mark Twain's indebtedness to Carlyle.[38] In this connection he points to some fundamental differences. Carlyle was "a conservative reformer, but critical even of his own reforms"; Mark Twain, on the other hand, was "more radical and the more radical, the more theoretical." Carlyle was a critic of parliamentary democracy; Mark Twain identified the American republic with democracy and held democracy to be the best possible form for the state.

[37] Walther Fischer (See *Englische Studien*, LXI, 137), on the other hand, feels that Mark Twain's philosophy would have become pessimistic even though he had never read a line of Goldsmith.

[38] *Op. cit.*, pp. 80-86.

Carlyle believed in the mission of great men in history and placed the great man in a certain antithesis to the masses; Mark Twain held that the masses produced the leaders. From his point of view, the republic and mass education are inseparably bound together. In their attitude towards the French Revolution he and Carlyle had opposing views. Whereas Carlyle held to the conviction that all the results of the revolution could have been attained without a revolution, Mark Twain accused only the "privileged classes" and insisted that they alone were culpable. These essentially different reactions do not exclude the possibility that Mark Twain did learn from Carlyle. It is not unreasonable, Schönemann points out, to trace Mark Twain's general conception of man as the product of history to a study of Carlyle. But Carlyle's estimate was too complicated and too metaphysical. What Mark Twain did was to simplify it to a mere contention that everything is only a dream, and, through his own processes of thought, to draw the conclusion that man is a machine, an impersonal engine. Carlyle's declaration, "there is no animal so strange as man," and his picture of the emptiness and baseness of human nature in the *History of the French Revolution* must have influenced Mark Twain in the pessimistic conception of mankind as evidenced in numerous works. Furthermore, his idea that crowns, scepters, and worldwide fame have no material value is connected with the metaphysical thinking of Carlyle, as is another favorite thought, expressed particularly in *The Mysterious Stranger,* that existence is merely a sequence of cause and effect beginning with the primal atom.

Whether Mark Twain's relentless struggle against the lie in all its forms was influenced by corresponding views expressed by Carlyle, is more difficult to sustain. Schönemann is of the opinion that an inner relationship exists, and he quotes passages from both authors to that effect; but he stresses the fact that Mark Twain, by nature of a rather violent temperament, frequently went too far, became too grotesque, and destroyed his art by too evident humor, as, for example, in his account of the behavior of the two tramps in *The Adventures of Huckleberry Finn.* Lüdeke,[39] on the

[39] *DL*, XLVI, 1811.

other hand, declares that Mark Twain's hatred of the lie, and his sympathy for the oppressed classes are impulses inherent in the character of the man himself and hardly to be attributed to Carlyle. Moreover, the American's interest in the social classes preceded that in the French Revolution.

Mark Twain must have known books by Carlyle other than *The French Revolution*. Schönemann lists the work on Cromwell as a source for *Death-Disk*, and *Past and Present*, a social study with its interesting comparison of Twelfth and Nineteenth Century England, as a model for *A Connecticut Yankee*. In contrast to Lüdeke,[40] he contends that the last is structurally based on a similar comparison. However, in view of Mark Twain's attitude towards the Middle Ages and the medieval church, he admits the possibility that Carlyle's treatment of medieval monasticism repelled him. Mark Twain also came to the conviction that the economic and moral state of the masses was a barometer of the condition of the country as a whole and Carlyle may have been a source for his ideas of the necessity of general education and of the organization of the working classes. However, Schönemann reminds us that Mark Twain was a radical revolutionary only in theory.

The many parallels Schönemann draws between Mark Twain and literary predecessors in an effort to disclose possible influences are in themselves interesting and informative. Nevertheless, they show the lack of scientific conclusiveness that is apt to mark this method of investigation. One finds it difficult to agree with his deductions as to literary influences.

It is generally accepted that Mark Twain had no profound or penetrating knowledge of history. It is Schönemann's opinion that he knew perhaps a little American and English history, but practically no European history, and that what he knew was derived not so much from study as from observation and assimilation "at second hand."[41] To bring out clearly the significance of Mark Twain's "pretty narrow range," Schönemann resorts to an inter-

---

[40] Lüdeke rejects Schönemann's view that *A Connecticut Yankee* is based upon the contrast between medieval and modern England. *Ibid.*
[41] *Archiv*, CXLIV, 204.

esting comparison with Theodor Fontane.[42] Mark Twain and
Fontane were alike in that they read "the wildest things . . . always
in reports of the police." Both were sharp observers, with contemporary history as the real life element. But there was a wide
difference in the character of their observations and in the manner
of reproducing them. Fontane delved deeply into historical studies
of Brandenburg and Prussia, and of France and England as well,
surpassing by far any knowledge Mark Twain may have had of
these countries. Even though Fontane did not spend a single day in
the United States, our critic credits him with as adequate a knowledge of North America as Mark Twain had of the whole of Europe.
Every journey deepened Fontane's impressions, while it merely
expanded those of Mark Twain. Fontane assimilated his good
and bad experiences so that they became a real part of his life;
Mark Twain confirmed his temporary impressions without being
inwardly affected. In the last analysis Fontane was a German and
a European, while Mark Twain remained an Anglo-Saxon. This
is clearly revealed particularly in their attitude towards England,
for while both condemned England with practically the same termi-
nology, the German Fontane adhered strictly to moral standards
of judgment whereas Mark Twain "twists and turns until he ar-
rives at tolerance and even a defense of dear old England."

One can hardly question Schönemann's assertion[43] that a just
evaluation of contemporary conditions presupposes a knowledge
of history and philosophy. A satisfactory understanding of history,
he continues, is quite impossible without a corresponding power
in philosophical thinking. Mark Twain's prejudices and prepos-
sessions and his intensity of feeling regarding all questions pertain-
ing to history, he attributes to a lack of just such a mental equip-
ment. Even at the present day the judgment of a modern American
regarding the political world and its history must be viewed in the
light of a self-reliant, ardent, and fervent republicanism which,
with the years, has become more and more intolerant and aggressive.

In treating Mark Twain's style as a phase of his literary per-

[42] *Ibid.*, pp. 204 f.
[43] *Ibid.*, p. 205.

sonality, Schönemann analyzes at some length the influence of Goldsmith.[44] This proceeded not from Goldsmith the novelist and author of *The Vicar of Wakefield,* for which Mark Twain had little or no understanding, but from Goldsmith the essayist and author of *The Citizen of the World.*[45] It is quite possible that some of the letters in *The Citizen of the World* may have influenced Mark Twain in his choice of subject matter. Parallels are drawn to show this relationship, but to the present writer they seem exceedingly forced and trivial. To be sure, there may be something in Schönemann's contention that certain of Goldsmith's ideas found a responsive chord in Mark Twain. The English author was a convinced patriot and a friend of the masses, and it may well have been that he passed on to Mark Twain some conceptions of English life and character. Goldsmith's comments on absurd and indecent books, as Schönemann points out, may have spurred him on to read all the works of which the Irish moralist disapproved. He may even have been impressed with Goldsmith's critical estimate of the French, in particular of Voltaire the satirist. But Schönemann's suggestion that Mark Twain's ideas of independence, frugality, and diligence were in some measure the product of his contact with Goldsmith awakens a reasonable skepticism. The mere fact that these ideals find an energetic expression in his letters does not necessarily imply that he derived them from Goldsmith. Such an hypothesis, Lüdeke contends,[46] has absolutely no value. In matters of technique and style Mark Twain may have learned from Goldsmith. Granted that the development of a style is a more or less mysterious and unconscious procedure, then Mark Twain may have been affected by the "colloquial ease" of Goldsmith's prose.

Goldsmith's principal influence, however, is found in the field of the essay. Schönemann prefaces his analysis of Mark Twain's essays with a discussion of the historical development of the es-

---

[44] *Op. cit.,* pp. 89-97.

[45] The subtitle reads *Letters from a Chinese Philosopher, residing in London, to his friends in the East.* There are some 193 essays in form of letters, newspaper articles with extracts from contemporary literature, particularly humorous descriptions of London's "sights." This book is an important landmark in the English revival of interest in the Orient.

[46] *DL,* XLVI, 1812.

say, and taking Mark Twain's *Sketches* as the basis of a comparison with Goldsmith's *Citizen of the World,* he finds a striking
similarity in subject matter and form.[47] To both he attributes
heterogeneous prose selections: character studies, humorous
sketches, satires on social conditions, characterizations of individuals as well as of the nation, anecdotes, fables, or dreams with
a moral application, in the form either of a sketch, a narrative, or
an essay of varied length. Mark Twain's essays, he points out, frequently assume the form of the newspaper letter, which was
gradually developed into the travel letter and then incorporated
as a chapter into one of his books of travel. This classification of
the letter as a form of essay he ascribes to Mark Twain's practice
of republishing letters in collections of essays. Considerable attention is devoted to the content of Mark Twain's essays, and an
attempt is made to understand his narrative style in the light of
his platform technique. His method consisted in writing as he
spoke. Though he shows a similarity to the English essayists in
that he speaks unassumingly, just as things occur to him, he
nevertheless uses a language fundamentally different, influenced
and formed by origin, custom, and design. Compared with that
of Addison and Goldsmith, Mark Twain's language is "unliterary." It has, however, a greater vitality, power, and freedom, and
these are attributed to its simplicity. This stands out clearly, particularly in contrast with Mark Twain's American predecessors
and contemporaries in the field of the essay.[48] Washington Irving's
style, with its emphasis upon "the choicest thoughts in the choicest
language," remained like that of the older essayists. Poe and
Hawthorne, in contrast, are more modern and more American.
With Poe, "effect" and "originality" go hand in hand, and beauty
is the essence of prose style. Hawthorne approaches the old essay
style in so far as he writes with a conscious moral purpose, as did
Addison and Goldsmith; but he is less biased, less affected, and
above all psychologically more penetrating. His style is lively and
clear, and penetrated with a real literary culture. Thoreau, on the
other hand, places the emphasis on absolute freedom and unre-

[47] *Op. cit.,* pp. 95-100.
[48] *Ibid.,* pp. 102 f.

strained liberty, on nature and the present. He strives for simplicity but his very personal style is careful and refined. Although Lüdeke does not categorically reject Schönemann's comparison, he nevertheless questions its accuracy.[49] In his opinion, Bret Harte and the journalism of the West should form the point of departure.

Among German scholars who reviewed Schönemann's work, there seems to be substantial agreement with his observation that Emerson was an early and influential enthusiasm. Schönemann finds a certain relation in the fact that both were "lecturers." Emerson was, to be sure, essentially a religious moralist and Mark Twain a humorist; but, as our critic observes, the humorist was also predominantly a moralist. In fact, he finds him more instructive than his listeners could have imagined, more than he himself frequently was aware of. The manner in which he informed the public was not less unique than that of Emerson. His most humorous lectures repeatedly reveal themselves as the most wonderful descriptions, as sermons, or soul-analyses. Lüdeke agrees with our critic that Emerson's influence extended over the entire succeeding generation and that Mark Twain certainly did not escape that influence.[50] But he rejects the parallels that are drawn as definitely inadequate.

Schönemann points to a strong resemblance in Emerson's and Mark Twain's philosophies of life.[51] Emerson's doctrine of self-reliance,[52] consistency, that is, "systematic consistency," and "self-culture" struck a responsive chord in Mark Twain and found a corresponding re-interpretation in his works, expressed of course in his own inimitable style. In their attitude and approach to the study of history both urged the student to read actively, not passively. But while Mark Twain agreed with and followed Emerson in the symbolic evaluation of facts, he rejected Emerson's view that "all history is sacred." Emerson's influence, our critic suggests, really lies in the fact that he directed Mark Twain's attention to the "falsification of traditional historical works," to their many absurdities, and to the genius of humanity, which is

[49] DL, XLVI, 1812.
[50] Ibid.
[51] Op. cit., pp. 106-112.
[52] Lüdeke rejects this assertion. DL, XLVI, 1812.

revealed in all history. In their approach to art both placed emphasis on the visual perception and on life as the source of all art. Both frequently make the impression of being iconoclasts; both, likewise, were accused of lacking an æsthetic sense. Mark Twain's interpretation of life that "everything is a dream," Schönemann would ascribe to Emerson. Mark Twain had found that idea in Carlyle, but, in our critic's opinion, it was Emerson who gave him the simpler interpretation. Emerson moreover stressed the importance of temperament. Mark Twain extended this doctrine of Emerson and added training and circumstance. Emerson, however, saved himself from the logical conclusion of his doctrine by stressing "the indifference of circumstance" and "the man is all," and thereby found refuge in optimism. Mark Twain, on the other hand, remained stranded in his pessimism. In the realm of religion, both were opposed to revealed Christianity, and both condemned the American Sunday-school. Both were sceptics, Mark Twain with "the defiant, somewhat blind consistency of the autodidact"; Emerson, on the other hand, was somewhat milder, for as Schönemann points out, he was "too well versed in European and particularly English and German philosophy to be so rigidly one-sided." Mark Twain, however, was almost aggressively anti-European in his Americanism. Emerson's ideal of the "gentleman" and of the relation between the gentleman and fashion were ideas, like that of Scott's "chivalry," totally alien to Mark Twain. Emerson was a "gentleman" by origin, tradition, and literary culture; Mark Twain, in contradistinction, "the self-made man in the self-made democracy," a democrat who never denied his western origin. Emerson was not a one-sided "follower of tradition." For him life was "neither intellectual nor critical-literary, but firm and coarse." Like Mark Twain, he had an understanding for manual labor. He was, however, "a very critical democrat, whereas Mark Twain was uncritical and fundamentally radical." Finally, in the matter of style, Schönemann alludes to a strong resemblance in their demands. Emerson emphasized "sincerity and marrow" in sentences, the "language of conversation transferred to a book," and words "vascular and alive." Though marked by an intensely concentrated expression,[53] his own essays were "full of turns from every-day life." Frequently the effect was commonplace; but in comparison with Mark Twain's "succulence and spontaneity," it had a feeble effect. Mark Twain, Schönemann concludes, is "bolder and more vigorous, without running the danger of becoming commonplace."

In the field of the "short story," Schönemann recognizes a tendency on the part of Mark Twain to conform to the same literary historical development as in the essay.[54] With numerous references to Mark Twain's works, he shows that in the treatment of "characters" Mark Twain has simply transplanted the essay technique to the short story. His great literary essays and his short stories were written in the 1890's and both were conceived "in the same literary mood and attitude of soul."

Any diagnosis of Schönemann's appraisal of Mark Twain as a literary personality would be incomplete if it failed to include his analysis of Mark Twain's *Weltanschauung*. As is well known, it has been a commonplace for critics to refer directly and indirectly to Mark Twain's utter contempt of mankind and to his pessimism as marked features of his thought. Those who saw primarily the humorist in him considered an investigation of this phase of his work superfluous; others, in view of the fact that his conduct was so in contrast with his theoretical expressions, sought to minimize it and to defend his philosophical efforts. In general, it may be said that Schönemann belongs to neither of these groups.

Accepting the philosophical narrative *The Mysterious Stranger,* the philosophical dialogue *What is Man?,* and *Mark Twain's Letters* as the basic expressions of Mark Twain's *Weltanschauung,* Schönemann takes up the charge of pessimism. He explains at some length the distinction between "unsystematic" pessimism and "systematic" pessimism and comes to the conclusion that in current popular thought, which defines pessimism as a mental attitude determined not on theoretical grounds but by the circumstances of the individual's life, his material situation, his bodily health, and

---

[53] Fischer also stresses the contrast between Emerson's careful style and Mark Twain's unliterary looseness of expression. Cf. *Englische Studien,* LXI, 139.

[54] *Op. cit.,* pp. 113-115.

his general temperament, Mark Twain was really pessimistic.[55]
His analysis, however, of Mark Twain's philosophical thoughts
concerning man, civilization, and the progress of the human race
convinces him that he was not a philosopher of pessimism. The
fact that he was not schooled in thinking, that he was self-taught
and realized clearly the disadvantage of his limited education; that
he, moreover, was an empiricist for whom sense perception constituted the origin and source of all knowledge and truth, pre-
cludes any possibility that he wished to suggest a philosophical
system or set up a complete intellectual world. Mark Twain then
had nothing to do with pessimism as a philosophy. His pessimism
is the result not of inner conviction, but primarily of external
experiences.[56] It was, however, definitely restricted by his practical puritanism. As an Anglo-Saxon he was a moralist who could
not refrain from voicing his objections against the existing world,
against injustice and pretext. Since he was "by temperament a
man who acted and then reflected," he became one of the most
effective propagandists of his time. With relentless determination
he worked for betterment in the world. Citing his efforts on behalf
of Helen Keller, Schönemann also accentuates Mark Twain's
struggle against "sham." It is particularly in this direction that he
gives indisputable evidence that "the pessimistic conception of life
cannot persist in the presence of purity and human kindness," for
therewith "all moral objections against life are restricted and
excluded from the subjectiveness of man."

That leads Schönemann to pose the question: "Did Mark Twain
achieve an intellectual victory over evil?" Measured in terms of
American intellectual life, he feels that Mark Twain's frank and
public recognition of evil was something great and commendable.
The critic concedes[57] that Mark Twain recognized the falsity and
danger of the view that "one merely needs to introduce the highest
form of human civilization, i.e., the American, into the world in
order to possess God's kingdom on earth." Although this recognition was occasionally obscured, he nevertheless never tired in his
effort to place his finger on the unjustified American optimism. He

[55] *Englische Studien*, LV, 63.
[56] *Ibid.*, p. 73.
[57] *Ibid.*, p. 75.

did not possess adequate intellectual powers to overcome the evil which he saw in various forms and "ended thus in hopelessness and despair, at least in his own thinking."

Our critic, however, is unable to find a definite solution in regard to Mark Twain's conception of fate. Whether fate represents absolute evil or absolute good (or both) he finds rather difficult to determine. Mark Twain is humorist enough to withdraw gracefully from the embarrassment, as for example, in *What is Man?* when he concludes that "his system of simple naked facts cannot deprive mankind of happiness." Only in *The Mysterious Stranger* did he have the courage to present his truth unadorned and to admit his philosophical helplessness without a smile or a jest.[58]

Yet even though our critic admits that Mark Twain's approach was serious and scrupulous, he nevertheless does not believe that the American author shared in the real life of the mind. That he seems inclined to attribute to his failure to realize that a pure or absolute "life of the spirit" really exists, and that the fundamental basis and fact of all real thinking lies in the ability to distinguish between "the temporal, material, conditional, imperfect life" (*dem Scheine*) and "the infinite, absolute, and perfect life of the reason" (*dem Sein*). Such a realization, Schönemann argues, might have led him "to the depths of the reflective life." In the last analysis, however, one might find the explanation in his Americanism, that "Americanism that evades all absolute philosophy and is content with a purely practical philosophy which rejects idealism in favor of a universal utilitarian doctrine."[59] What really prevented Mark Twain from attaining a deeper *Weltanschauung* without special philosophical insight and training, was the fact that he was not at heart religiously inclined. His intuition would otherwise have led him to further perception when his sober reason failed him. He lacked inner vision; he only "saw" with his eyes, only very seldom did he think, like poets, with his heart. Consequently Schönemann finds only a few warm heart throbs in his works. *Joan of Arc,* the one book planned, thought out, and written out of the fulness of his heart, is cited to show his own attitude toward religion.

[58] *Ibid.,* p. 77.
[59] *Ibid.,* p. 79.

In regard to the religious consciousness of Mark Twain, Schöne-mann feels that he did not live *nach innen* and that his own personal inner life did not lead him to a union with God. Religion did not constitute a living inner force or give rise to an unconstrained sincere piety. Whether he can be called religious will depend on the interpretation of the concept "religion." If one considers religion and morality synonymous, then Mark Twain was religious, for he led a moral life and sought to practice what he taught seriously or humorously. On the other hand, he rejected the entire foundation of Christianity, and expressed his doubts about all religion in general. He was on the whole hostile to orthodox Christianity, as was Voltaire. But with his growing negation of all circumscribed religion, he eventually disregarded all conformities to convention. The fact that his wife and friends[60] remained faithful to him in spite of all religious differences, testifies to his humanity and uprightness.

At this point it may be well to summarize briefly Schönemann's findings. First, in his discussion of the literary personality of Mark Twain he takes cognizance of the thesis that dominated the literary thinking of the time—that Mark Twain was a divided and frustrated personality, whose potentially great creative power was stifled by his family and social entanglements. Although he does not accept the final conclusions of Brooks' arguments, he nevertheless does not offer a convincing refutation.

Second, in the development of Mark Twain's humor the West is held to have played a dominant rôle, for it gave him the material, the method, and the inspiration. Even after he left the West he remained under the influence of this "Western humor" for a long time. Tragic personal experiences, however, intensified by an innate tendency towards melancholy and bitterness, deepened, enlarged, and consecrated that humor.

Third, Schönemann establishes the invalidity of the general conception of the "ultra-original," "unliterary" Mark Twain. He rejects the common view that his genius "just grew like Topsy" and that he was "lacking in book-learning." He stresses the fact that

[60] Mark Twain's spiritual health, Schönemann holds, demanded opportunities for intimate expression. His friendship with Howells permitted him for years to express himself quite freely on religious issues.

he was acquainted not only with American and English literature, but also with the classical works of French and German literature. The author's extensive reading, attested to by the many references and citations in the works themselves, was supplemented by the broadening influence of his numerous travels and wide range of acquaintances. Contrasts and parallels are drawn, but there is a diversity of opinion regarding the specific influence of the individual authors discussed.

Fourth, Schönemann points out that Mark Twain was by nature romantically inclined, but that his romantic nature frequently came into conflict with his anti-romantic tendencies. This conflict within Mark Twain himself, between his romantic nature and his constitutional pessimism and negating materialism, between Mark Twain the romanticist and Mark Twain the realist, explains the strange paradox resulting in the author's acceptance of Cervantes and rejection of Walter Scott. Parallels are again drawn to show the relation to Cervantes, but there remains the open question, as Schönemann suggests, to what extent "the conscious imitation of Cervantes' *Don Quixote* was responsible for the suppression of his own romantic instincts." Mark Twain's attitude towards Scott is cited as sufficient proof that the American had no understanding of the value of romanticism as a cultural experience for America as it had been for Europe.

Fifth, for his philosophy of history Schönemann stresses Suetonius, Lecky, and Samuel Pepys, but particularly Carlyle's *History of the French Revolution*. Comparisons are drawn to show possible influences, comparisons which are vigorously rejected by some of Schönemann's critics, and it is a question how far one is willing to go in accepting the influence of Carlyle's work. Mark Twain's view of history and his conception of social interrelations and the great social problems are alleged to have been extended and deepened through the intellectual contact with Carlyle.

Sixth, Mark Twain's essay style, it is pointed out, was influenced by that of American and foreign essayists who preceded him— by Goldsmith, Addison, Montaigne, Emerson. These influenced him not only in his ideas, but also in his presentation, which was always realistic. The influence of Goldsmith is not universally accepted by Schönemann's reviewers; there is general agreement, however, regarding that of Emerson. Although Mark Twain seems to have conformed to the general development of the essay, he nevertheless "trod his own path and created his own laws." In view of his background, Schönemann stresses the fact that Mark Twain was to a certain degree unique in his use of the English language. His fine ear and his long experience as lecturer and author enabled him to distinguish between the English and the American language. He is generally characterized as "a master of the simple and straightforward style."

Seventh, Mark Twain's attitude towards mankind and the universe is characterized as the result of an individual pessimism. But this pessimism is attributed not to inner philosophical convictions, but to purely personal experiences. On the whole, Mark Twain is not recognized as a profound thinker or systematic philosopher. Schönemann points out the flaws in his philosophical system, and emphasizes that Mark Twain was conscious of his own inadequate intellectual powers and consequently did not wish to develop a philosophy; that he was unable to suggest a solution of life's problems; that he tried to solve it on the secular level and failed; that a lack of a deeply religious consciousness prevented him from seeking a supernatural solution. The ideas of his philosophy are interesting, not for their originality, but for the flavor with which he expressed them.

Schönemann's constructive contribution to the understanding of the American author in Germany, particularly in the years from 1920 to 1925, entitles him to recognition, as Lüdeke suggests, for introducing Mark Twain into German *Anglistik* and as the foremost Mark Twain critic in Germany. For while there are many German writers who, following the general interpretation of the mass of readers, stressed just one phase of the author's work, for the most part its humor, it was Schönemann who pleaded consistently for a deeper understanding of all the phases of Mark Twain's literary personality "as the human and spiritual basis of his collective activity." All of this assures him of a unique position among the many German scholars and critics who have occupied themselves with the American writer and justifies the space which we have given to his contribution.

VII

GRADUAL DECLINE OF INTEREST
1926-1932

Publications, 1926-1927——Evaluation of Mark Twain's works: Bauch, Fischer, Sastre, Krebs, Harbeck——Publications, 1928——von Jan's appraisal of Mark Twain's *Personal Recollections of Joan of Arc*——Reduction in publications, 1929-1932——Birkenfeld: Analysis of wit and humor——Helen Keller——Brattskoven——Summary.

There is reason to assume that Schönemann's study of Mark Twain, coupled with the reviews of it, helped to intensify interest in the American author. Even though the character of Schönemann's approach to the author may be criticized, no one is likely to question that the results of his investigation are highly suggestive or that they were a challenge to German scholars for further research. Nevertheless, there is little in the following years to show that they did act as a spur to productive effort. German writers who in the past had commented on Mark Twain were for the most part largely inarticulate; and those who did contribute an article or so in this decade cannot be credited with new analyses. Their observations constitute, at most, a reiteration of earlier opinions.

This lack of a creative interest among German critics does not mean that the public at large was indifferent. German publishers still found it profitable to issue Mark Twain volumes, and the publication of certain works is, in some measure, a very rough gauge of the public appreciation. In 1926 the "Weltgeist-Bücher"[1] of Berlin added a volume of some sixty-three pages of *Humoristische Skizzen;* Hesse and Becker a volume each of *Tom Sawyers Abenteuer und Streiche*[2] and *Huckleberry Finns Abenteuer und Fahrten;*[3] and the Weidmannsche Buchhandlung of Berlin a fourth printing of the school edition of *The Prince and the Pauper,*

[1] These comprised a series of some three hundred and ninety volumes, at prices from sixty-five pfennig up. The translation of the Mark Twain volume was prepared by a Margarete Kraus.
[2] Vol. XLVI of the series "Die Schatzkammer." This series appeared between 1926 and 1930, and consisted of some one hundred and ninety-six volumes.
[3] Vol. XLVII of "Die Schatzkammer."

prepared and edited by Dr. E. Lobedanz.[4] The year 1927 was slightly more productive. H. Fikentscher of Leipsic brought out a volume[5] of sketches, entitled *Humoresken;* the Buchhandlung des Stenographenverbandes Stolze-Schrey, a volume of some ninety-six pages of *Ausgewählte Skizzen* in shorthand; Loewe of Stuttgart found *Der Prinz und der Bettelknabe*[6] in sufficient demand to justify an *edition de luxe;* Velhagen & Klasing added an abridged school edition[7] of *The Adventures of Tom Sawyer*, prepared by Hermann Perschmann; the Zenith-Verlag of Leipsic issued a volume of *Die Abenteuer des Tom Sawyer und Huckleberry Finn*,[8] and the Aschendorffsche Verlagshandlung of Münster i. W. selected Mark Twain's essay on *Cecil Rhodes* for its edition[9] of extracts from Thomas Hardy, S. R. Crockett, James Payn, and Mark Twain. Two literary anthologies appeared which may have found considerable circulation in educational institutions: the one, *Englisches Lesebuch zur Einführung in Kultur- und Geistesleben. Teil 2. Die Literatur der Vereinigten Staaten von Amerika*,[10] compiled by Dr. Reinhold Bauch, a member of the board of national education in the Staats-Gymnasium in Jena; and the other a "Handbuch der Literaturwissenschaft" bearing the title *Amerikanische Prosa. Vom Bürgerkrieg bis auf die Gegenwart* (1863–1922),[11] prepared by Walther Fischer, at that time

[4] Consideration for the abilities of the post-bellum school generation compelled Lobedanz to shorten the text.

[5] This extensive work of some three hundred and sixteen pages was incorporated as a volume of the "Hafis-Lesebücherei." A *Nachwort* is appended to the text and emphasizes the author's varied life. The text itself was revised by Lotte Blaschke who collaborated on this work with Dr. Georg Witkowski, the "geistiger Leiter der Hafis-Bücherei." In more recent years she has interested herself particularly in the contemporary social and cultural problems of America.

[6] This was the seventh edition and contained eight full-page plates and twenty-eight text illustrations by Willy Planck.

[7] Vol. LVII of the "Sammlung französischer und englischer Schulausgaben." This volume added an introduction and notes by Douglas Yates, lecturer in English at the University of Breslau.

[8] The "Zenith-Bücher" included works from such authors as Boccaccio, Casanova, Gorki, Goethe, Schopenhauer, Dumas, and Dostoyefsky. The translation of the Mark Twain volume was prepared, with a preface, by Walter Keiler.

[9] Issued as a volume of "Aschendorffs Moderne Auslandsbücherei."

[10] Dresden: Ehlermann, 1926. Mark Twain is represented by two extracts: one dealing with student life from *A Tramp Abroad*, the other from *The Adventures of Huckleberry Finn*.

[11] Leipsic: Teubner, 1926. Fischer's selections include *The Notorious Jumping Frog of Calaveras County*, two extracts from *The Mysterious Stranger*, and one from *The Adventures of Huckleberry Finn*.

professor of English philology in the Technical Institute in Dresden. Both of these works contained literary appraisals of Mark
Twain's work, and these, augmented by the opinions of reliable
commentators in various articles during these two years, constitute additional links in that body of opinion which seeks to cultivate a balanced understanding of Mark Twain and his art.

There seems to be no disagreement among these critics on Mark
Twain's function as a satirist, moralist, social critic, and narrator,
and his achievements in these directions are duly, though briefly,
recorded, with varying emphasis. One is conscious, however, of a
rather distinct cleavage of opinion in regard to Mark Twain's humor. Kurt G. Krebs, for example, discounts and belittles Mark
Twain's "humor of exaggeration" as not representative of genuine,
true humor. He is inclined to prefer the somewhat "more subtle
comedy" of such books as *Humorous Travels through Texas* by
Sweet and Knox; for the exaggeration of the latter pertains to
the improbable, the less credible, while that of Mark Twain in-
volves the impossible. In fact, he places the humor of a Washington Irving in his *Sketchbook* and *History of New York by David
Knickerbocker* far above that of a Mark Twain.[12] On the other
hand, Hans Harbeck, poet, critic, and essayist, values Mark
Twain's humor more highly. Accepting the American author as
"the master of American humor" and *"in puncto* humor still the
holder of the world's record," he underscores the view that Mark
Twain was not a "funny man" but a writer for whom humor was
a vehicle to express his *Weltanschauung* and *Sittlichkeit*.[13] Also
interesting is the ranking of individual works of Mark Twain. *The
Adventures of Tom Sawyer* and *The Adventures of Huckleberry
Finn* are recognized as powerful, realistic epics, as an American
panorama, "equally remarkable in its perfection of detail as in the
extent and magnitude of the whole." Fischer is inclined to accept
the former, with its extensive play of the artistic imagination and
its wholesome and cheerful atmosphere, as the author's masterpiece;[14] Bauch, on the other hand, is disposed to follow American
appraisement in granting preëminence to the latter in spite of all

[12] *Hellweg* (Essen), August 10, 1927, p. 245.
[13] *Der Kreis* (Hamburg), Jg. IV, 1927, p. 276.
[14] Fischer, *op. cit.*, p. 41.

its eccentricity and its sombre and oppressive mood.[15] On the whole there is agreement among the commentators on the value of the *Sketches*. Enrique Sastre, an outstanding journalist of Düsseldorf, for example, finds them "his most intellectual, definitely most typical work"; but in contrast with the large majority of German observers, he is inclined to subordinate the value of *Roughing It*, which he translates as *Auf der Walz*, on the ground that other writers have given a far superior factual account of the West.[16]

It is but natural that, with the passage of years, German critics should face the question of Mark Twain's ultimate service to literature and to succeeding generations. There is a strong impulse at this time to emphasize the supremely important positive value of his work as a painter of the American pattern of life, as shown by his broad descriptions of customs in the Middle West and in the novels of the Mississippi.[17] These, it is declared, constitute his most distinctive contribution to literature,[18] and form "the foundation of his European fame as narrator and humorist."[19] His work, in the considered opinion of another critic, must be judged "as a whole, in spite of all contradictions inherent in his character"; to do justice to him as a man of letters, it must be approached not as an agreeable entertainment to while away a few hours now and then, nor should it be regarded too seriously "as a source for psychological, philosophical, or sociological study." The European reader, this critic continues, must simply "yield to the author's captivating genius," and then the desired effect will not be wanting.[20]

Beginning with 1928, however, there is a noticeable decline in publications and articles of a critical nature, a decline that becomes more marked as the years pass. In number of volumes, 1928 brought only three: a volume[21] of *Tom Sawyers Abenteuer*

[15] Bauch, *op. cit.*, p. 110.
[16] *Volksbühnen-Blätter,* Jg. III, 1926, pp. 102 f.
[17] For example, *The Adventures of Tom Sawyer, The Adventures of Huckleberry Finn, Life on the Mississippi,* and *Puddn'head Wilson.*
[18] Cf. note 15 above.
[19] Cf. note 14 above.
[20] *Volksbühnen-Blätter,* Jg. III, 1926, p. 103.
[21] This edition was limited to members of the "Gesellschaft für Literatur."

by the Leuchtfeuer-Verlag of Hamburg, and two volumes of sketches: the one a new Reclam edition of some eighty-eight pages of *Ausgewählte Skizzen*,[22] the other a collection of humorous sketches and travel pictures by Hesse & Becker bearing the title *Lustige Gefährten—tolle Sachen. Erzählungen und Skizzen.*[23] Only one work received critical consideration in this year, the *Personal Recollections of Joan of Arc,* a work which has been ignored, with a few exceptions, by German critics, even though some of these conceded that it deserved recognition. This novel appeared in the Tauchnitz edition as early as 1896; but in all the years that followed there seems to have been no demand for a German translation. One may perhaps find a reason for this lack of interest in the fact that this poignant tragedy was predominantly localized in France. Perhaps the subject matter was too intimately known to the German reader to create a genuine interest. For that reason even the rather brief analysis of Eduard von Jan, lecturer in the University of Würzburg, assumes sufficient importance to warrant notice. In his discussion of "Das literarische Bild der Jeanne d'Arc" in the *Beihefte zur Zeitschrift für romanische Philologie,*[24] von Jan defines the relative position of Mark Twain's work within the framework of the literary picture of Joan of Arc from 1429-1926. In his judgment Mark Twain's novel represents "the standard work of American Joan literature";[25] at the same time it is "an irony of intellectual history" that America, devoid of tradition, should have produced a novel in the Nineteenth Century dealing with the most sacred epoch of French tradition, and that the serious, sublime character of Joan should have appealed to one of the most celebrated humorists. Characterizing Mark Twain's romance as "ein Nachläufer der Romantik,"[26] von Jan points out, by way of explanation, that the romanticists had turned more to the "enigmatical and problematical nature of the material," that they tried to grasp, explain, and judge the character of Joan by the spirit and standards of the

[22] Translated by Mira v. Hollander-Munkl.
[23] Vol. CXLVII of "Die Schatzkammer."
[24] Heft 76; pp. 139-143.
[25] *Ibid.,* p. 187.
[26] *Ibid.,* p. 144.

Middle Ages, that they sought new individual traits in the comprehensive mass of historical facts and endeavored to create works that would be equally significant from the historical and poetical standpoint. Nevertheless, their attempt "to reconcile truth with poetic intuition" did not have positive results. "The sublimity and particularities of the historical facts" did not permit a "reorganization," but merely "a subsequent emotional experience." Mark Twain followed the traditional interpretation and did not attempt a new creation in the character of Joan. Though, like his French contemporaries, he thus adheres to historical tradition, he nevertheless to a certain degree retains his artistic freedom by introducing an intermediary character as an eye-witness of the events, thereby "transforming a purely historical romance into a *Zeitroman*."

That the Mark Twain vogue was gradually suffering an eclipse becomes apparent particularly in the final four years of this decade. In 1929 only two volumes appeared. Hesse & Becker offered a reprint of *Lustige Gefährten* which included a biography and a brief epilogue by Ludwig Fürstenwerth, and the Buchgemeinde of Berlin a volume of *Tom Sawyers Abenteuer.*[27] Aside from a reprint of *Tom Sawyers Abenteuer und Streiche* and *Huckleberry Finns Abenteuer und Fahrten*[28] by Hesse & Becker, the year 1930 brought only an English version of Mark Twain's *The Death-Disk,*[29] by the Moritz Diesterweg firm. As far as can be ascertained,[30] nothing was published in 1931, and only one volume in 1932, which was in the nature of an anthology, by the Deutsche Buchgemeinschaft of Berlin.

This work bore the interesting title *Das Lächeln des Weisen. Die schönsten Humoresken,*[31] and contained some 409 pages of selections from Mark Twain's works which might be supposed to

[27] Translated by R. Freund.

[28] These two volumes had appeared in 1926 as part of "Die Schatzkammer."

[29] Vol. CLXXXI of "Diesterwegs neusprachliche Lesehefte," a series of some one hundred and eighty-one volumes of English and French authors. Mark Twain's story of fifteen pages was edited and prepared by Dr. Friedrich Meyer, Oberstudienrat in Lübeck, and sold for thirty pfennigs.

[30] In this connection it should be noted that the Robert Lutz firm of Stuttgart released new issues of works which had already appeared with its imprint, but it is impossible to date them accurately.

[31] The illustrations were furnished by Hans Koischwitz.

be of interest to contemporary Germans. In deference to contemporary taste, Günther Birkenfeld, the translator of the work and an author in his own right,[32] found it expedient to abbreviate and to mollify the grotesque exaggerations, in the hope that such revisions would heighten and increase their effectiveness. The translation was prefaced by a carefully reasoned appreciation which identifies and traces the factors that governed the development of Mark Twain. On the whole, most of Birkenfeld's observations are based upon the work of his predecessors, for example, Schönemann and Paine; but his introduction renders an important service in that it sets forth more clearly than hitherto the full import of Mark Twain's evolution as a humorist. German criticism in the past had alluded repeatedly to Mark Twain's wit and humor without seeking to define the limitations of each. Using anecdotes from the author's childhood and old age as a basis for his analysis,[33] Birkenfeld is the first to develop an evaluation of the author out of a careful examination of the distinction between wit and humor. Wit, he argues, is "the faculty of quick perception and association." The witty individual, gifted with an unusual imagination and powers of swift perception chooses among various possibilities the one which does not occur to any one else and expresses it so as to produce an amused surprise. This procedure is "perfectly logical and correct," for "the real secret of wit lies in the fact that it asserts an impossibility or a grotesque improbability against which one can advance no logical objection." Wit is thus "a *logical* attitude"; humor, on the other hand, "a *human* attitude." Humor is "the wit of the heart." The witty individual becomes a humorist when "the special heart tones of kindness and love as well as of doubt and resignation pervade his powers of wit." Young Clemens, our critic points out, revealed the necessary requisites of genuine humor early in his childhood: an appealing kindliness of heart, an infallible sense of justice, and an intuitive love of truth. The sobering perspective of the years and the tragic personal experiences which awakened and intensified his inclination toward melancholy and bitterness then deepened, enlarged, and consecrated that humor which, in the last analysis,

[32] Birkenfeld is known primarily for his sketches and novels.
[33] Introduction, pp. 10-21.

is "a mild smiling at the finite in contemplation of the infinite and the eternal" and implies "moisture" and "tears through which one smiles." *The Adventures of Tom Sawyer* and *The Adventures of Huckleberry Finn* give ample evidence of that. But the most perfect example of the highest form of humor, that is, the humor of irony, he finds in the story of *Captain Stormfield's Visit to Heaven,* which introduces the anthology. Here, he contends, Mark Twain reveals himself as the master in the exercise of "that superior smiling play with human concepts and wishes," as a master in the art of "demolishing apparent earthly values by means of supernatural standards of measurements."

Within these last four years Mark Twain's name did not disappear entirely from the German press. Though negligible as criticism, there is one article that can not be lightly set aside, for it is unquestionably of merit for the framing of a composite picture of Mark Twain. On January 15, 1930, the *Unterhaltungsblatt* of the *Münchener Post* published a vivid portrait of Mark Twain by Helen Keller.[34] In this article, "Mark Twain, wie ich ihn kannte," Helen Keller draws from her personal association and brings in many little incidents and sidelights. She does not pretend to view Mark Twain with impersonal detachment; instead, as the context abundantly shows, she is a devoted friend writing of one whom she deeply loved and admired. Her account of her experience when reading *Eve's Diary* with him, we may assume, must have appealed to the German reader, both for the mere facts and for its absolute sincerity of tone. The picture which she draws of Mark Twain as a magnanimous and noble personality with a warmth of sympathy and a depth of human understanding for the physically handicapped may appear, at first sight, to add nothing new to what was already known of the author, but its effect on the German mind will probably not be overlooked by any future investigator. German criticism, indeed, is coming more

[34] Helen Keller is recognized the world over as a shining example of what a steadfast will can actually accomplish in the face of almost insuperable disability. In 1929 she published her book *Midstream; my later life.* The Robert Lutz Nachfolger, Otto Schramm Verlag in Stuttgart issued this work in a German translation under the title *Mitten im Lebensstrom.* It contained a chapter on her friendship with Mark Twain, and this the *Braunschweigische Landeszeitung* republished on January 12, 1931. The content of this article is practically identical with that mentioned in the text above.

and more to the conclusion that it is extremely difficult to form a conception of the nature of Mark Twain without testimony from his contemporaries.

With a single exception, the twentieth anniversary of Mark Twain's death passed practically unnoticed. Even the lone article in the *Fränkische Tagespost* of April 22, 1930, by Otto Brattskoven, entitled "Mark Twains Erscheinung. Zu seinem 20. Todestag am 21. April," confines itself primarily to an enumeration of the elements that form his humor and to a bringing together of many incidents designed to illuminate his character; for this critic, like many of his predecessors in Germany, is convinced that Mark Twain's complex personality is not fully revealed in his books. These must be supplemented by the personal reactions and observations of the man himself. Although many of his descriptions are said to retain a certain vitality for the readers of the present day and age, Brattskoven nevertheless insists that his work has not escaped the fate of becoming the type of classic that the author himself feared to be when he remarked that only "that book is classic that everyone praises but no one reads." Notwithstanding that, the critic feels that Mark Twain will long be remembered and that he will hold a permanent position in the record of American literature.

On the basis of the evidence just presented, we may conclude, with some degree of finality, that Mark Twain's popularity in Germany, in so far as it finds definite expression in the press and in publications, is gradually on the decline. As a whole the amount of critical study and comment expended on him in this period is quantitatively quite insignificant and qualitatively less important than that devoted to certain other foreign writers. Yet it contributed its share to the enlightenment of the public mind and obviously helped the process of educating German opinion on Mark Twain. This decade brings new confirmation of a fact which has been noted in preceding years, that the *Sketches*, *The Adventures of Tom Sawyer*, and *The Adventures of Huckleberry Finn* are the works preëminently in public demand in Germany. That these works, years after the passing of their author from the scene, still find repeated publication is evidence of the peculiar and lasting character of their appeal to the German mind.

VIII

CENTENNIAL APPRECIATIONS, 1935

Commemorative exercises——Analysis of German reception of Mark Twain's humor——Mark Twain's significance for American culture——Mark Twain's friendship for Germany, Austria, and Switzerland——Basis of Mark Twain's abiding reputation——Mark Twain and the future generations——Summary.

German interest in Mark Twain in the final years of our study, 1933-1937, revolves almost exclusively about the year 1935. That year marked the one hundredth anniversary of the birth of Mark Twain. As was only natural in a country in which he enjoyed a great vogue, the occasion was by no means overlooked.[1] Appropriate commemorative exercises were arranged,[2] though on a much smaller scale than in America and elsewhere. The German press paid tribute to him with special articles. Numerous journalists, authors, and literary critics summarized his extraordinary individual qualities and his picturesque career,[3] with its wide oppor-

[1] Even prior to November 30, 1935, Bruno Manuel, a German feuilletonist and author of extravaganzas and satires, contributed a prelusory article *Im Schatten des Titanen* to the *Leipziger Neueste Nachrichten* (September 17, 1935), in which he called attention to the great centennial celebrations in America. He takes note of the absurd extremes to which American correspondents go in order to satisfy the curiosity of the American people. Not least among these is the effort to interview contemporaries of Mark Twain in whose memory he still lived. Manuel then introduces us to one of these contemporaries, who dwelt in the shadow of the "Titan." This was an American resident in Berlin, the illustrator, Paul Richards. Richards belonged to the old guard of American illustrators, and was known as the *Leibzeichner* of Mark Twain. His sketches immortalized the author-humorist in a way in which the books could not; they give us a picture of a legendary figure, with the leonine locks, the drooping mustache, the fierce bushy eyebrows, and the string tie. Manuel's article is, therefore, a tribute to Richards and his contribution to the permanent visual record of Mark Twain.

[2] The German celebration of the Mark Twain centenary was sponsored by the Carl Schurz Society. It was held on December 2, 1935 in Berlin. Participating in these ceremonies were the American Club, the American Women's Club, the American Chamber of Commerce, the American section of the English Seminary of Berlin University, the German Institute for Foreigners, and the Amerika Institut. Ratsherr Protze, representing the city of Berlin, delivered a brief address of welcome and was followed by the American Ambassador to Germany, Dr. W. E. Dodd, who spoke briefly on Mark Twain the man. Professor Friedrich Schönemann of the University of Berlin delivered the principal address on "Mark Twain und Deutschland." Twelve of Richards' portrait-sketches were placed on exhibition.

[3] An article signed H. W. S. in the *Deutsche Zukunft* (December 1, 1935, p. 15) deals almost exclusively with Mark Twain's life, stressing particularly the youthfulness of his art.

tunities. Others brought him vividly into the reader's consciousness through anecdotes[4] by him and about him, while several who had had the good fortune to know him contributed anecdotal reminiscences.[5] It would be inaccurate to say, however, that German publishers showed a similar interest. The Mark Twain centennial year, as a matter of fact, brought only a pamphlet[6] of some forty-eight pages, *Erzählungen,* published by Velhagen & Klasing. Other volumes appeared between 1933 and 1937, but with one exception[7] they were all reprints.[8]

Broadly speaking, the centennial comments do not essay a novel interpretation or a new appraisal of Mark Twain, nor do they analyze the conflicting views regarding his personality and work. Casual reference is of course made to the paradoxes in his character, to the melancholy and pessimism which was a marked feature of the man, and to the theory that he was frustrated in his ultimate development by the conflicting forces within and in his environment.[9] On the whole, however, the greater part of the

[4] Sophie Droste-Hülshoff (pseudonym: E. Trost), translator, essayist, and novelist, contributed a number of anecdotes to the *Königsberger Tageblatt* of November 29, 1935. These give the reader an insight into Mark Twain's personality and reveal the various elements that make up his wit and humor. The reader is left to make his own synthesis. The American illustrator, Paul Richards, also furnished some anecdotes to the *Bibliothek der Unterhaltung und des Wissens* (LX; 171-175). These picture Mark Twain as a *Propagandachef* during his editorship of the *Buffalo Express.*

[5] The anonymous author of an article in the *Schwäb. Merkur* (November 24, 1935) pays tribute to two important living contemporaries of Mark Twain. The one is Paul Richards, the other the prototype of the German student who was immortalized by the humorist in *A Tramp Abroad,* the Prussian Landrat a. D. Herr von Flügge, from Speck, Kreis Naugard. Flügge studied in Heidelberg in 1878 and was a member of the "Korps Saxo-Borussia." Mark Twain became acquainted with him and described a *Mensur* in which Flügge participated.

[6] Nr. 270 of the series "Neusprachliche Lesebogen." This volume was edited by Heinrich Gade.

[7] In 1936 Williams of Berlin issued a volume of some 503 pages, entitled *Die Abenteuer des Tom Sawyer und Huckleberry Finn.* It was translated by Ulr. Johannsen and Marie Schloss, and illustrated by Walter Trier.

[8] By 1935 Diesterweg was able to issue a fifth edition of Mark Twain's *The Death-Disk.* The Lutz firm of Stuttgart also found it possible to reprint certain volumes of the non-illustrated edition of 1892 and of the six-volume edition of *Humoristische Schriften. Neue Folge* of 1903.

[9] In his discussion of *Mark Twain's Notebook* (New York: Harper, 1935), Schönemann reiterates his rejection of the "superstition" of modern critics that the censorial influence of Mrs. Clemens, or his friend Howells, or the *kulturlose* America had prevented Mark Twain from "having his say." Mark Twain's fiery

German critics seems to avoid scrupulously all controversial issues. Apparently mindful that the centennial was to be a celebration, the critics occupy themselves with reviewing Mark Twain's unique significance for the general direction of American culture and literary history, and seeking to determine which of his works had enduring value.

Mark Twain's fame, it is generally conceded, demonstrates conclusively that American humor, in its infinitely diverse and extremely varied forms, has in him its most comprehensive embodiment. Concerned chiefly with the German reaction toward this humor, the commentators make much of the point that the German reader, accustomed to look for "the life-bestowing moisture of the heart" in the works of a Fritz Reuter or a Peter Rosegger, can very easily become indifferent and apathetic. The fact, however, that the German public at large received Mark Twain's humor so well is attributed, in some quarters at least, primarily to the intellectual and literary kinship between German and American humor and to the inner relationship between the German and the American character.[10] Mark Twain, it is stressed, had an unusually sympathetic understanding of the German soul— that is, of the German character and nature. He possessed the genuine Germanic trait, according to the critic Lossow,[11] of being able to do what the consecrated of all religions term *die Lichter umstellen*, that is, "to think with the heart and to feel with the mind." With him it was a matter of origin, for he was of English and Dutch descent. His humor consequently combines "a Celtic-pointed, Gallic-spirited direction with the dry wit of the Low-German."[12]

The studied examination of Mark Twain as a humorist also leads our commentators to a review of the forces which are held to have given direction to his artistry. These may be summarized briefly as follows: first, inheritance. His "warm humanity and

---

temperament had to be curbed; but his love of truth, supplemented by his satire and humor, compelled him to give expression to his feelings. Schönemann agrees with Paine in his conclusion that "Mark Twain had his say." See *Die Neueren Sprachen,* XLIV, 264.

[10] Schönemann, *Deutsche Allgemeine Zeitung,* November 24, 1935.

[11] *Berliner Börsen-Zeitung,* November 29, 1935.

[12] Werner Lenz, *ibid.*

geniality of heart" and his tendency to view the world objectively in terms of humorous contrasts are traced directly to his mother.[13] Second, his Southern training, which reflected itself in the breadth of his "mental horizon," in a certain sovereign attitude toward life, and in his sense of chivalry.[14] Third, the Puritanism of the East, which exercised such a tremendous dominance over the social views and practices and which necessarily came into conflict with the West, with its unfettered existence and creative possibilities for the individual, its independent mastery of life and humanity.[15] And fourth, the aggressive, extravagant, and reckless pioneer life in the Middle West (the crossroads of the nation), with its intense struggle for existence.

Of all these forces, in the judgment of the German critics, it was predominantly the frontier life of the West that gave him the material and the technical methods. Schönemann, in his discussion of recent Mark Twain studies in America,[16] calls attention particularly to two works that explore the frontier—Bernard De Voto's *Mark Twain's America* (Boston, 1932) and Minnie M. Brashear's *Mark Twain, Son of Missouri* (University of North Carolina Press, 1934). He is inclined to agree with their thesis that the frontier life was the greatest force in shaping Mark Twain's genius. He subscribes particularly to Miss Brashear's conclusions that Northeast Missouri was not a misfortune nor a tragedy but "ein gutes Geschick," an exceptionally favorable environment for the training of Sam Clemens; that the life in Hannibal with its Seventeenth and Eighteenth Century European cultural elements gave his genius essence and character; that Mark Twain was perhaps unacademic but not unliterary. He stresses also her conclusion that it was a combination of the Western and Southern influences that made him "a border ruffian from Missouri." On the other hand, he rejects the view of Fred Lewis Pattee, the American literary historian and a founder and editor of *American Literature,* who in the 1935 edition of his anthology (*Mark Twain. Representative Selections with Introduction and*

---

[13] Paul Feldkeller, *Leipziger Neueste Nachrichten,* November 30, 1935.
[14] Schönemann, *Hochschule und Ausland,* XIV, 38.
[15] Hanns Martin Elster, *Rheinisch Westfälische Zeitung,* November 27, 1935.
[16] *Die Neueren Sprachen,* XLIV (1936), 267 ff.

Bibliography. New York: American Book Co., 1935) contends that "the literary comedian, the humorous personality," is the creation of "the trans-Mississippi West," while "the author, the creator of classical-literary works" is the special product of the East. Schönemann admits that Howells assisted constructively in Mark Twain's literary development, but he maintains that Howells himself was "Mid-Western." And Mrs. Clemens' inspiration, Schönemann suggests, did not make him "Eastern." Pattee's conclusion—"The Mark Twain that has endured was born in New England"—he feels is exaggerated and unjustified.

As regards his humor, the centennial writers find that Mark Twain joined the tradition of the literary comedians and sought escape in burlesque humor and grotesque satire. Humor thus became an escape from the bitterness of life, a relaxing counterbalance against the struggle for existence, a mental adjustment,[17] a safety-valve. This was then supplemented by a realization of the conquering mission of the humor of the heart with its healing, redemptive qualities. Thus Mark Twain's humor developed into a universally accepted humor.

Even though these German critics are accustomed to associate wit and humor with Mark Twain, they nevertheless consider it a grave mistake to think of him only in such terms. They feel that the German reader sacrifices something precious in the personality of Mark Twain if he accepts him as merely a funny man or buffoon who interested and amused the masses. The humorist in Mark Twain is only one phase, which must not be magnified in utter disregard of other equally important phases. Werner Lenz perhaps expresses the German view most effectively when he asserts that it would be more prudent to look upon Mark Twain as an "interpreter of the human soul."[18]

In estimating further Mark Twain's position and his significance for American culture, our German commentators seem fairly certain that he will ever remain a foremost interpreter of a truly great Americanism. Four essentially vital qualities dominated him and the youth of his country: cheerfulness, impartiality, fair-

[17] Walther Fischer, *ibid.*, XLIII, 473.
[18] Cf. note 12 above.

ness, and fearlessness. These he brought into immediate and vital reality and embodied in a few immortal figures. Frank Thiess, author and critic, an honorary vice-president of the Mark Twain Society in the United States in 1930, terms these characteristics "ingredients" of an Americanism which helped to establish the greatness of the United States in the second half of the Nineteenth Century.[19]

It is therefore not surprising that the more penetrating observers should be practically unanimous in the view that Mark Twain's most distinctive contribution lies in his rôle as a "realistic chronicler of an important era of original American life." The era of Mark Twain, these point out, was a period of unimaginable progress, of complex industrial development, all of which he personally experienced. *Life on the Mississippi*[20] and *Roughing It*[21] are specifically cited in this connection as incomparable products of individual experiences, so permeated with variety and vivacity that those works will always endure as permanent documents of reality.[22] Even after forty years *Meine Reise um die Welt* still appeals to some of the German critics for its freshness and invigorating atmosphere.[23] To others the lucid and illuminating *Sketches* contain such clearly defined and discriminating portraits of community life which spanned that vital formative period in American history that they too are expected to retain significant value as serious cultural criticism and as an impressive inquiry into the ways of American life.[24] For the reader of the present day, their charm lies in the expression of a natural vitality and affirmation of life and in the inimitable literary style, which is distinctly individual.

Mark Twain's interest in and understanding of the usages and traditions of others causes a number of critics[25] to refer to him

[19] *Königsberger Allgemeine Zeitung*, November 30, 1935.

[20] Schönemann calls this work "das herrlichste Erlebnis- und Heimatsbuch, ein Kulturdokument." (Cf. note 10 above.) And Frank Thiess finds it and *Roughing It* unusually appealing as biographical works and artistic masterpieces. (*Königsberger Allgemeine Zeitung*, November 30, 1935.)

[21] *Ibid.*

[22] Cf. note 15 above.

[23] Cf. note 19 above.

[24] G. A. Walter-Rottenkamp, *Kölner Volkszeitung*, November 30, 1935.

[25] Schönemann, *Die Neueren Sprachen*, XLIV, 268; Fischer, *ibid.*, XLIII, 4-5.

as a rich source for the folklorist and to agree with Dr. West[26] that he had a "scientific interest in folklore." The folklore element, so perceptible in the portrayal of the life and customs in the communities along the Mississippi, in the speculations in land, in the descriptions of Negro superstitions and popular customs, shows how inseparably Mark Twain is bound up with his America.

Finally, Mark Twain is also important for American literary and cultural history as the representative of a new kind of Americanism in its attitude towards the Old World.[27] Walther Fischer in particular brings this view to the fore. He explains that Mark Twain advocated and demanded recognition of American standards of measurement. As an exponent of contemporary progressive America he united diverse cultures,[28] and with remarkable self-assurance and all the prejudices of a young democrat judged the older cultures and monarchies. The European reader, our critic admits, finds it difficult to understand fully the impertinent boldness with which he evaluates the religious, historical, and aesthetic values of the Old World. However, the placing of modern American civilization over against European culture should be interpreted more or less as a masked glorification of the spirit and life of the New World.[29]

Throughout the centennial appreciations there runs a note of genuine affection, and what one might almost describe as "cordiality under restraint." The German critics, almost without exception, are happy to express their profound gratitude to Mark Twain as one of the few prominent Americans of his time who displayed a real interest in Germany,[30] Austria, and German Switzerland,[31]

[26] Victor R. West: *Folklore in the Works of Mark Twain* (Lincoln, Nebraska: University of Nebraska Studies in Language, Literature and Criticism. No. 10, 1930).

[27] Fischer, *Die Neueren Sprachen*, XLIII, 477; H. M. Elster, see note 15 above.

[28] For example, in *The Innocents Abroad, A Tramp Abroad*, and two historical phantasies, *The Prince and the Pauper* and *A Connecticut Yankee*. The first of these, Fischer feels, owes its success primarily to the fact that it was timely, the popular expression of a definite "intellectual situation."

[29] *Die Neueren Sprachen*, XLIII, 477 f.

[30] Cf. note 24 above.

[31] In honor of Mark Twain's centennial, Dr. August Hüppy (see Chapter V, note 32) published a commemorative work in German, *Mark Twain und die Schweiz, dem grossen Freund und Bewunderer unseres Landes zum 100. Geburtstag gewidmet.* (Zurich: Reutimann & Co., 1935). It is not a critical analysis of Mark Twain's work, but predominantly an appreciation of Mark Twain as the greatest

and a friendship for them. With pardonable pride they recall the unusually considerate attitude of their countries as hosts to this distinguished American on his frequent visits. They are equally proud of the fact that their lands formed a basic source for some of his works. They point to his descriptions in such works as *A Tramp Abroad* as permanent documents of an observing and deeply sympathetic mind. His shrewd understanding of the German national soul, so vividly shown in his praise as well as condemnation of the German character, landscape, and language, contributed considerably, as the critic Thiess expresses it, to setting aside many misconceptions of the world regarding them.[32] In his criticism of the German language, in which he had an inexhaustible interest, he is even credited with having assisted, in his own way, in the evolution of a healthy and sound *Sprachgefühl*.[33]

The reflection on Mark Twain's friendship for Germany leads some of the critics who had followed Mark Twain criticism closely to draw parallels between him and certain German authors. Schönemann, for example, asserts that Mark Twain's *Weltanschauung* was influenced by Schopenhauer; that his conception of the meaning and value of laughter offers an instructive parallel to that of Wilhelm Raabe, for "a certain spiritualized optimism" seems to have permeated both in their early years. With Wilhelm Busch he shared "a Germanic passion for the grotesque," "an inimitable linguistic artistry," and a certain "criticism of life." Both Mark Twain and Busch, it is noted, are still frequently quoted in their native lands for their humorous and striking phrases and maxims.[34]

It can not be said that the centennial commentators subscribe

---

glorifier of the Alps. His visits to Switzerland for travel, recreation, and work in 1878, 1891, and 1897 are affectionately recalled, and *A Tramp Abroad* and the travel letter, *Switzerland, the Cradle of Liberty,* with Switzerland as background, are reviewed. The emphasis throughout is placed on the passionate enthusiasm with which the American humorist interpreted the weaknesses and the strength of Switzerland. Dr. Hüppy based his work on the biographies by Howells and Paine, on Mark Twain's correspondence with Howells, on the notes of Twichell, and on the works themselves. His work adds nothing of importance to the facts established and set down elsewhere.

[32] *Königsberger Allgemeine Zeitung,* November 30, 1935.

[33] Cf. note 24 above.

[34] *Deutsche Allgemeine Zeitung,* November 24, 1935; Tim Klein in *Münchener Neueste Nachrichten,* November 30, 1935.

wholeheartedly to the view, advanced repeatedly by some sections of German opinion, that Mark Twain was a systematic thinker and a philosopher. The observations at this time, in fact, are on the whole quite reserved on this particular point. Among some of the critics the impression prevails that he had no remarkable intellectual talents, that his ideas emanate rather from a "nervously active, even seismic intelligence," and that these ideas are neither keen nor systematic.[35] Among others, however, there is clearly a disposition to look upon him as a "philosophical character."[36] Still others by their silence would seem to suggest disapproval of any attempt at analysis of the philosophy of a man like Mark Twain.

More emphatic expression, however, is given to the opinion, found especially in the critic Tim Klein, dramatist and dramatic critic of the *Münchener Neueste Nachrichten,* that Mark Twain is a *Dichter,* a creative writer.[37] Defining creative ability as the power to interpret life and to delineate a definite national character with originality of style, Klein finds sufficient evidence to warrant the conclusion that Mark Twain fulfills the requisites of a creative artist in every respect. The feeling seems to predominate that the author's reputation will rest upon his power as a pathetic and realistic narrator, and not so much upon his early successes as upon the two books which interpret with sympathetic understanding the spirit of boyhood.[38] In view of the artistic narrative power which fashioned and vitalized everything in *The Adventures of Tom Sawyer* and *The Adventures of Huckleberry Finn* with living reality, the critic Willinsky[39] goes so far as to assert that these two stories approach the great works of universal world literature. In no other work, he contends, does Mark Twain attain such freedom of "spiritual poise," such "philosophical content of humor," and such "a charm of genuine writing."[40]

[35] Hans Bütow, *Frankfurter Zeitung,* November 30, 1935.
[36] Paul Feldkeller, *Leipziger Neueste Nachrichten,* November 30, 1935.
[37] *Münchener Neueste Nachrichten,* November 30, 1935.
[38] *Ibid.;* also Hans Langkow, *Bibliothek der Unterhaltung und des Wissens,* LX, 171.
[39] *Magdeburger Zeitung,* November 30, 1935.
[40] Frank Thiess finds these two works "schwer geniessbar" for adults. In fact, he is inclined to minimize their importance and to stress those works which con-

There is very little diversity of opinion as to Mark Twain's significance for the present and for future generations. The German reader of today, it is generally agreed,[41] finds much in Mark Twain that is outmoded and antiquated, but also much that still remains as a supreme contribution to the joy of living. It is hoped that as generations come and go they will cherish his name and fame. Walther Fischer, in his concluding remarks,[42] offers something of a synthesis of the German attitude when he suggests that in years to come Mark Twain should be remembered for his "great wealth of literary forms of expression," his engaging and picturesque characterizations, and his "moral pronouncements"; that he should remain the great moralist who, rooted deeply in the ideal of American democracy, experienced the antitheses in human existence and embodied these, according to his mood and inclination, in his best works; who mastered them as an American pragmatist, for whom the difficulties of life exist only to be overcome. It is in the realm of human relationships that his abiding power will be felt; for here the reader, provided he reads intelligently and intensively, will recognize the wisdom, the melancholy, and the quality of his rich, free, and responsive humanity.

In the light of the analysis here presented, the German centennial critics seek to serve the memory of Mark Twain by reminding their readers of their debt to an outstanding personality who rendered great services to his contemporaries, and to subsequent generations. Though yet too near him to appraise him with cold exactitude, they nevertheless seek to define his place in American cultural and literary history, and reëmphasize the enduring quality of his work. Individually and in the aggregate, the somewhat formidable number of centennial acknowledgments is a reminder that his work still has many devoted admirers in Germany and that with the passage of the years it seems quite unlikely that the name of Mark Twain will ever fade out of German memory.

---

tain descriptions of the Mississippi, of the West, and of his world travels, such works as *Life on the Mississippi* and *Roughing It*.

[41] Rudolph v. Losow, *Berliner Börsen-Zeitung*, November 29, 1935.

[42] *Die Neueren Sprachen*, XLIII, 478 f.

CONCLUSION

An investigation of the reception of Mark Twain in Germany and of the history of the progressive development of his vogue there reveals a situation far from simple and one not exactly easy to appraise. Many complicated and interlocking factors, such as political, social and economic as well as personal ideas and habits, enter in, some of them far removed, others more immediate and easily discernible. Not individually but collectively they assist in explaining the direction of the German attitude toward Mark Twain.

The popularization of Mark Twain in Germany, as evidenced by the wide distribution[1] of his works in that country from 1874 to 1937, was brought about primarily by the combined efforts of the publishers, many of whom were comparatively insignificant. In the very early years of the pre-war period it was possible to interest only a small circle of readers in his eccentric humor; the German public as a whole definitely rejected it. The steadfast persistence, however, of certain German publishers who maintained an unwavering faith in the solid achievements of the American writer enabled him to take deeper root there. Other publishers, whether for cultural or commercial reasons, then incorporated him into their libraries and assisted in extending the knowledge of Mark Twain beyond the confines of the more highly educated class. The steadily mounting number of publications justifies the

[1] It is practically impossible to ascertain the exact number of Mark Twain's books which have been published and circulated in Germany. According to information supplied the writer, many of the publishing firms have gone out of business. Others have destroyed their records, while still others refused to release their data. Nevertheless it is possible to hazard a minimum estimate. On the basis of the available figures, German publishers (from 1874-1937) sold at least 425,000 copies of the *Sketches*, 240,000 of *The Adventures of Tom Sawyer*, 190,000 of *The Adventures of Huckleberry Finn*, 58,000 of *Life on the Mississippi*, 50,000 of *Puddn'head Wilson*, 24,000 of *The Prince and the Pauper*, 53,000 of the *Reisebilder*, 28,000 of *Adam's Diary*, 23,000 of *Tom Sawyer Abroad*, 80,000 of *Roughing It*, 18,000 of *The Man that Corrupted Hadleyburg*, 30,000 of *More Tramps Abroad*, 34,000 of *A Tramp Abroad*, and 16,000 of *Tom, der kleine Detektiv*. Adding to these figures at least 8,000 copies more which represent other works—works which appeared in only one edition—it becomes probable that the total number of volumes of Mark Twain's works actually *sold* in Germany has reached well over a million.

conclusion that beginning with 1892 Mark Twain's popularity among the widely varied reading public rose gradually and reached a high point approximately in 1910. From 1910 to the outbreak of the World War his popularity remained undiminished. With the great conflict and its economic difficulties there came a lull and a temporary abatement of interest. The establishment of the republic in 1918 and the rise of a spirit of liberal education created a more favorable atmosphere for a better understanding of Mark Twain, his art and philosophy, which the German adult of the pre-war period, grounded in veneration for monarchism, was unable to appreciate.[2] The spirit of independence and of a true democratic equality in the works of the American author were bound to make a powerful impression on the first generation of the new German republic.[3] The humanitarianism of the American people in saving millions of German children from starvation drew attention first of all to America as the Promised Land and then perhaps to literary works that would enable Germans to understand the American scene and the pattern of American life. The interest of the children in the juvenile books of Mark Twain may have aroused that of parents and that, in turn, may have led to an interest in his other works. The early years of the post-war decade advanced the popularity of the American humorist until the year 1923 when, it may be said, he attained the rank of a best seller in Germany and with it a popularity unheard of in the case of a foreign author. Steindorff characterizes that as the "Mark Twain year" in Germany. Beginning with 1929, however, there has been a gradual decline in the public sale. In the years immediately following Germany was in too great turmoil to have more than fleeting thoughts about America. Although articles and books on this subject and discussions of America began to reappear after the National Socialist regime had been in power for some time and its propaganda had been set to work to give the German nation a new ideology, there was no noticeable reawakening of Mark Twain sentiment. There has been, indeed, a very marked falling

---

[2] Ulrich Steindorff expresses it quite aptly: "They either would or could not understand Mark Twain's smiling philosophy or his satiric mockery or his relieving laughter." Cf. *The New York Times Book Review*, July 13, 1924.

[3] Steindorff refers to Mark Twain as "praeceptor Germaniae." *Ibid.*

off since 1933.[4] The fact that the centenary (1935) of the birth of Mark Twain was not marked by the publication of a centenary edition of his works suggests perhaps that if such an edition had been issued, its sales would have been disappointing, for there was no evidence of any widespread demand for it.

On the basis of the publications the works that ranked highest in popular interest throughout the years under discussion are the *Sketches, The Adventures of Tom Sawyer*,[5] and *The Adventures of Huckleberry Finn*. These will in all probability survive as works of art. However, the popularity of these particular books must be attributed in the first place to their subject-matter, and in the second place to the favorable circumstance of copyright. These works appeared in Germany prior to 1892, the year in which the copyright law with America went into effect. Consequently publishers in Germany could still bring them out freely without paying a royalty. This fact may partially explain the unusual number of firms that issued these volumes.

In view of the vogue of Mark Twain in Germany, German criticism, taken as a whole, comprises a body of writings strikingly uneven in quality. Most of the pre-war material consisted of brief reviews; and in these it was impossible to do more than touch on one or another aspect of the author's books. However, although much of the most informed criticism written about Mark

---

[4] The attempt to identify Mark Twain as a Jewish author may have had some effect. Even as early as 1910 we find a reference to *Salomon* Clemens in an obituary article on Mark Twain by Sigmar Mehring; and in 1927 Kurt G. Krebs (*Hellweg*, Essen, Aug, 10, 1927, p. 245) speaks of Mark Twain as "der aus den ehemaligen habsburgischen Gebieten eingewanderte Jude." The impression that he was of Jewish extraction received extensive circulation in the *Handbuch der Judenfrage* by Theodor Fritsch (Leipsic: Hammer Verlag, 1933, 32nd ed.). In an article on "Das Judentum im ausländischen Schrifttum" by Alfred Eisenmenger (pseudonym of a well-known and reputable scholar in Germany), we find this comment: "Man will nicht glauben, dass Mark Twain Jude ist; aber seine Schreibweise ist jüdisch." It was found, however, impossible to substantiate this contention and consequently this remark has been deleted from the later editions.

[5] Although the American Mark Twain films—*The Adventures of Tom Sawyer, The Adventures of Huckleberry Finn, A Connecticut Yankee*, and *The Prince and the Pauper*—did much to sustain an interest in Mark Twain in America, they played no rôle in the popularization of that author in Germany. *The Adventures of Tom Sawyer* was in fact the only Mark Twain film distributed in Germany. Produced by the Paramount Film Co. in 1931, it was shown in practically all the larger cities, but with very little success. The screened story may have stimulated the sale of the book from which it was taken, but its showing had probably no influence on the appreciation, in Germany, of Mark Twain as a writer.

Twain appeared in literary magazines that served only a small and select circle, it formed as a whole a distinct contribution to the growing literature about the American writer. Its general tone is an acceptance of his positive merits as an interpreter of the American mind.

Throughout the years conflicting appraisals run parallel. In general, however, it may be said that Mark Twain was the object of more praise than censure. There was always, to be sure, an undercurrent of hostility which not infrequently caused critics to refer to America with a turn of phrase that would be irritating to Americans; but this prejudice did not dominate German opinion at any given period. In some instances there is good reason to believe that these comments and criticisms arose from a feeling of annoyance and resentment that so much praise should be showered upon an American author.

In the early years of Mark Twain's introduction to the German public, humorists were in the foreground on both sides of the Atlantic. German critics consequently emphasized the humorous elements in his work and regarded humor as the primary phase of his art. They analyzed it into its component elements and represented it as the embodiment of all the characteristics which are inherent in the "American humor." Comparisons are frequently drawn between American and German humor. For the most part, these are to the disadvantage of American humor and the negative qualities of the latter are stressed. Critics in Germany, however, gradually came to realize that humor was not the most essential element in Mark Twain's art but only a means to express his philosophy. Mark Twain, accordingly, is not merely a humorist to amuse the masses but a philosopher, a moralist, a satirist, a reformer, a sociologist. This serious approach to the American author was by no means universal; it was rather limited to a few writers. German critics of the pre-war period were, on the whole, still predominantly interested in the content, in the subject-matter of the individual works and seemed to underestimate his outstanding literary qualities. However, their interest in his individual works led them to an attentive consideration of Mark Twain the man. His unique career, his multiplex personality and its altogether human qualities are constantly recalled, so that it is difficult to say which had the great fascination for the German mind, his life or his work.

With the post-war period German criticism takes a more scientific aspect. It tends more and more to approach Mark Twain as a literary personality that demands serious consideration. It does not deny the wholesome character of his humor. There were indeed many critics who still esteemed him primarily as a humorist. But more informed minds, following the leadership of Schönemann, recognized the inadequacy and injustice of categorizing him as merely a humorist. These insisted that his humor could not be isolated from the rest of his literary personality. Mark Twain's position in American culture and his significance for the German reader as a valuable source of information about America were clearly set forth by German centennial commentators.

Nevertheless, in spite of the increasingly informed and serious character of the critical opinion of his work, in popular tradition Mark Twain was, is still, and promises to continue to be the humorist. Anecdotes and stories constantly tend to strengthen the public in its belief that he was a sort of clown of specifically American taste.

Under the present material, political, and spiritual conditions in the national life of Greater Germany today, it is extremely questionable whether Mark Twain's books will continue to find a market. Although the American writer left, beyond question, his impress on a large circle of friends in the Germany of the past, his aims and ideas, it may be said, do not in general accord with the psychology of the present generation. It would therefore seem that he will have fewer and fewer readers. However, with an improved book market it is not impossible that his fame may revive to some extent, as his work has certain characteristics that appeal to the German reader and probably will continue to do so in spite of all passing ideologies and modes. These are qualities of "the fantastic and grotesque," of "the wildly primitive," and the tendency toward melancholy, which with "persistent idealism" and "bohemianism" go to make up the picture of Mark Twain which German criticism has fashioned.

APPENDIX I

GERMAN TRANSLATIONS OF MARK TWAIN'S WORKS
1874-1937

(in chronological order)

1874 Jim Smileys berühmter Springfrosch und dergleichen wunderliche Käuze mehr. Im Silberlande Nevada. Deutsch von Moritz Busch. Leipzig: Grunow. 408 S. ("Amerikanische Humoristen," Bd. II).

1875 Die Arglosen auf Reisen. Deutsch von Moritz Busch. Leipzig: Grunow. 406 S. ("Amerikanische Humoristen," Bd. IV).
Die neue Pilgerfahrt. Deutsch von Moritz Busch. Leipzig: Grunow. 395 S. ("Amerikanische Humoristen," Bd. V).

1876 Das vergoldete Zeitalter. Roman von Mark Twain und Charles Dudley Warner. Deutsch von Moritz Busch. 2 Teile. Leipzig: Grunow. 315, 352 S. ("Amerikanische Humoristen," Bd. VI und VII).
Die Abenteuer Tom Sawyers. Deutsch von Moritz Busch. Leipzig: Grunow. 314 S. ("Amerikanische Humoristen," Bd. XI).

1877 Skizzenbuch. Deutsch von Moritz Busch. Leipzig: Grunow. 467 S. ("Amerikanische Humoristen," Bd. XII).

1878 Ausgewählte Skizzen. Deutsch von Wilhelm Lange. Bändchen 1-6. Leipzig: Reclam, 1878-1897. ("Universalbibliothek," Nr. 1019, 1079, 1149, 2072, 2954, 3749).

1886 Unterwegs und Daheim. Neue Sammlung humoristischer Skizzen. Deutsch von Udo Brachvogel, M. Jacobi, G. Kuhr und anderen. Stuttgart: Lutz. vii & 312 S. ("Sternbanner-Serie," Bd. II).

1887 Fürst und Bettler. Frei nach dem amerikanischen Original des Mark Twain. Deutsch von Josephine Flach. Konstanz: Verlag der "Deutschen Heimat." 180 S.

1888 Leben auf dem Mississippi. Deutsch von A. Brachvogel und F. Siller. Stuttgart: Lutz. xvi & 317 S. ("Sternbanner-Serie," Bd. V).

1890 Die Abenteuer und Fahrten des Huckleberry Finn. Deutsch von Henny Koch. Stuttgart: Lutz. vi & 321 S. ("Sternbanner-Serie," Bd. VIII).
Heitere Liebesgeschichten. Von Mark Twain, L. Koelle, O. v. Oberkamp und H. Bäcker. Leipzig: Verlag der Zehnpfennig-Bibliothek. 64 S. ("Zehnpfennig-Bibliothek," Nr. 1).
Der Prinz und der Betteljunge. Eine Erzählung für die Jugend jeden Alters und Geschlechts. Deutsch von Helene Lobedan. Giessen: Ricker. xi & 339 S. mit 156 Illustrationen.

1892   Mark Twains ausgewählte humoristische Schriften. 25 Lieferungen. 6 Bände. Stuttgart: Lutz.

    I. Tom Sawyers Streiche und Abenteuer. Deutsch von Margarete Jacobi. 281 S. 42. Auflage, 1935.

    II. Abenteuer und Fahrten des Huckleberry Finn. Deutsch
von Henny Koch. 320 S. 39. Auflage, 1934.

    III. Skizzenbuch. Deutsch von Margarete Jacobi, Henny Koch
und L. Ottmann. 285 S. 34. Auflage, 1935.

    IV. Auf dem Mississippi. Lehr- und Wanderjahre. Nach dem
fernen Westen. Deutsch von Margarete Jacobi und L.
Ottmann. 300 S. 27. Auflage, 1926.

    V. Im Gold- und Silberlande. Lehr- und Wanderjahre.
Deutsch von M. Jacobi und L. Ottmann. 224 S. 28.
Auflage, 1935.

    VI. Reisebilder. Anhang: Mark Twains Lebensgeschichte.
Deutsch von M. Jacobi und L. Ottmann. 288 S. 28.
Auflage, 1935.

Der amerikanische Prätendent. Roman. Stuttgart: Deutsche Verlagsanstalt. viii & 310 S.

1893   Skizzen. Aus dem Englischen von H. Löwe. Leipzig: Bibliographisches Institut. 327 S. ("Meyers Volksbücher," Nr. 991-
995).

1897   Die Millionenpfundnote. Humoreske. In Gabelsberger Stenographie übertragen und autographiert von Adolf Schöttner.
Neustadt: Marnet. 56 S. ("Büchersammlung für Gabelsberger
Stenographie," Nr. 37).

Die Million-Pfund-Banknote und andere Erzählungen. Mit 25
Illustrationen von R. A. Jaumann. Berlin: Hillger. 127 S.
("Kürschners Bücherschatz," Nr. 46).

1898   Ausgewählte humoristische Schriften. *Illustrierte Ausgabe.* 6
Bände. Stuttgart: Lutz.

    I. Tom Sawyers Streiche und Abenteuer. Illustrationen von
H. Schrödter. 307 S. mit Bild des Verfassers. 22. Auflage,
1919.

    II. Abenteuer und Fahrten des Huckleberry Finn. Illustrationen von H. Schrödter. 351 S. 18. Auflage, 1921.

    III. Skizzenbuch. Illustriert von H. Schrödter. 318 S. 12.
Auflage, 1918.

    IV. Auf dem Mississippi. Lehr- und Wanderjahre. Nach dem
fernen Westen. Illustrationen von H. Schrödter und Albert Richter. 320 S. 10. Auflage, 1909.

    V. Im Gold- und Silberlande. Lehr- und Wanderjahre. Illustrationen von A. Richter. 316 S. 11. Auflage, 1912.

    VI. Reisebilder. Anhang: Mark Twains Lebensgeschichte. Illustrationen von H. Schrödter. 318 S. 11. Auflage, 1914.

Meine Reise um die Welt. Autorisierte Übersetzung von Margarete Jacobi. Stuttgart: Lutz. 478 S. 3. Auflage, 1900.

Der junge Detektiv und andere Kriminalgeschichten. Von Mark Twain und Edgar Allan Poe. Nach dem Englischen bearbeitet von Hans Helling. Berlin: R. Jacobsthal. 163 S. ("Amerikanische Detektivromane," Bd. VI).

Der Querkopf Wilson. Roman. Autorisierte Übersetzung von Margarete Jacobi. Stuttgart: Lutz. 280 S. ("Sammlung ausgewählter Kriminal- und Detektiv-Romane," Bd. XIX).

2. Aufl., 1899; 3. Aufl., 1901; 4. Aufl., 1903; 5. Aufl., 1906; 6. Aufl., 1909; 14. Aufl., 1935.

1899   Tom Sawyers Streiche und Abenteuer. Stuttgart: Lutz. 281 S. ("Eisenbahn-Ausgabe").

Skizzenbuch. Stuttgart: Lutz. 285 S. ("Eisenbahn-Ausgabe").

Die Abenteuer und Fahrten des Huckleberry Finn. Stuttgart: Lutz. 320 S. ("Eisenbahn-Ausgabe").

1900   Tom Sawyers Abenteuer. 2 Bände. Deutsch von Thomas Bürk. Mit Illustrationen von W. Roegge. Berlin: Hillger. 128, 124 S. ("Kürschners Bücherschatz," Nr. 176-177).

Die Abenteuer des Tom Sawyer. Deutsch von H. Hellwag. Mit einer Einleitung von Franz Kwest und dem Bilde des Verfassers. Halle: Hendel. iv & 194 S. ("Bibliothek der Gesamtliteratur des In- und Auslandes," Nr. 1413-1415).

Im Gold- und Silberland. Stuttgart: Lutz. 295 S. ("Eisenbahn-Ausgabe").

Leben auf dem Mississippi. Nach dem fernen Westen. Stuttgart: Lutz. 298 S. ("Eisenbahn-Ausgabe").

Reisebilder. Stuttgart: Lutz. 246 S. ("Eisenbahn-Ausgabe").

Querkopf Wilson. Wie die Stadt Hadleyburg verderbt wurde. Zwei Erzählungen. Autorisierte Übersetzung von Margarete Jacobi. Stuttgart: Lutz. 384 S. 2. Auflage, 1901. Aus dem Handel gezogen.

1901   Erzählungen und Plaudereien. Aus dem Englischen von H. Löwe. Leipzig: Bibliographisches Institut. 207 S. ("Meyers Volksbücher," Nr. 1285-1287).

König und Betteljunge. Frei nach dem Englischen von Helene Stökl. Wien: Pichler. 81 S. ("Bücherei für die Jugend." Hrsg. von Josef Ambros. Bd. XXI).

Adams Tagebuch und andere Geschichten. Autorisiert. Stuttgart: Lutz. 275 S. Aus dem Handel gezogen.

Tom, der kleine Detektiv. Nebst zwei Erzählungen von Bret Harte. Autorisierte Übersetzung von Margarete Jacobi. Stuttgart:

Lutz. 200 S. ("Sammlung ausgewählter Kriminal- und Detektiv-Romane," Bd. XXV).

3. Aufl., 1903; 4. Aufl., 1907; 5. Aufl., 1908; 6. Aufl., 1916; 7. Aufl., 1918.

1902 Die Abenteuer Huckleberry Finns. Deutsch von H. Hellwag. Mit Einleitung von Franz Kwest und dem Bilde des Verfassers. Halle: Hendel. iv & 236 S. ("Bibliothek der Gesamtliteratur des In- und Auslandes," Nr. 1577-1579).

1903 Des Treulosen Ende. (A Double-Barrelled Detective Story). Autorisierte Übersetzung. Berlin: Jakobsthal. 218 S. ("Amerikanische Detektiv-Romane," Bd. XXVIII).

Mark Twains humoristische Schriften. Neue Folge. 6 Bände. Stuttgart: Lutz.

> I. Tom Sawyers neue Abenteuer. Tom Sawyer im Luftballon. Tom, der kleine Detektiv. Autorisierte Übersetzung von Heinrich Conrad und Margarete Jacobi. 304 S. 18. Auflage, 1926.
>
> II. Querkopf Wilson. Übersetzung von M. Jacobi. 280 S. 13. Auflage, 1926.
>
> III-IV. Meine Reise um die Welt. Übersetzung von M. Jacobi. 346, 330 S. 13. Auflage, 1926.
>
> V. Adams Tagebuch und andere Erzählungen. Übersetzung von H. Conrad. 303 S. 13. Auflage, 1926.
>
> VI. Wie Hadleyburg verderbt wurde. Nebst anderen Erzählungen. Übersetzung von M. Jacobi. 320 S. 12. Auflage, 1926.

1904 Tom Sawyers Abenteuer und Streiche. Jugendausgabe. Stuttgart: Lutz. 307 S. ("Mark Twains humoristische Schriften für die Jugend").

4. Aufl., 1919; 7. Aufl., 1931.

Huck Finns Fahrten und Abenteuer. Jugendausgabe. Stuttgart: Lutz. 351 S. ("Mark Twains humoristische Schriften für die Jugend").

6. Auflage, illustriert und mit Abbild, 1931.

1905 Prinz und Bettler. Frei nach dem Amerikanischen von Rudolf Brunner. Illustriert von G. A. Stroedel. Leipzig: O. Spamer. 176 S.

2. Aufl., 1908; 3. Aufl., 1911.

Die 1,000,000 Pfundnote und andere humoristische Erzählungen und Skizzen. Leipzig: M. Hesse. 94 S. ("Hesses Volksbücherei," Nr. 226).

Tot oder lebendig. Erzählungen und Skizzen. Leipzig: M. Hesse. 94 S. ("Hesses Volksbücherei," Nr. 237).

Prinz und Bettelknabe. Eine Erzählung für die reifere Jugend.

Deutsch von Helene Lobedan. Mit 36 Illustrationen von Willy Planck. 2. Auflage, Stuttgart: Lutz. viii & 236 S. 3. Aufl., 1910; 4. Aufl., 1921; 6. Aufl., Prachtausgabe mit 8 Vollbildern und 28 Textillustrationen, 286 S., 1927; 12. Aufl., 255 S., (Loewes Jugend-Bücher) 1937.

1906 Mark Twain: Wie Tom den Zaun anstrich. Stuttgart: Lutz. ("Lutz Kriminal- und Detektiv-Romane," Bd. XLVII). 2. Aufl., 1907; 3. Aufl., 1908; 4. Aufl., 1916.

1909 Die Abenteuer Tom Sawyers. Mit einer Einleitung von Albert Erding und dem Porträt des Verfassers. Berlin: A. Weichert. 300 S.
Die Abenteuer Huckleberry Finns, des Kameraden von Tom Sawyer. Mit einer Einleitung von Albert Erding und dem Porträt des Verfassers. Berlin: A. Weichert. 347 S.

1910 Mark Twains Werke. Auswahl in drei Bänden. Übersetzung von Margarete Jacobi, Henny Koch und L. Ottmann. Nachwort von Dr. Ludwig Fürstenwerth. Leipzig: Hesse & Becker. ("Romane der Weltliteratur"). Neudruck, 1925.
    I. Humoristische Skizzen. Reisebilder. Lebensbeschreibung Mark Twains. 172, 174 S.
    II. Tom Sawyers Abenteuer und Streiche. Die Millionpfundnote und andere Erzählungen. 285, 93 S.
    III. Huckleberry Finns Abenteuer und Fahrten. Tot oder lebendig und andere Erzählungen. 333, 93 S.
Die Abenteuer Tom Sawyers. Ausgewählte Skizzen. Deutsch von H. Hellwag. Berlin: F. Schulze. 96 S. ("Sammlung berühmter ausländischer Schriftsteller." In vereinfachter deutscher Stenographie, System Stolze-Schrey, hrsg. von Fr. Schulze. Serie I, Bd. IX).

1911 Tom Sawyer als Detektiv. Wie es Huck Finn erzählt. Mit Bildern von Theodor Volz. Stuttgart: Neues literarisches Institut. 68 S. ("Saturn. Illustr. Universal-Bibliothek," Bd. VI).
Ausgewählte Werke. 6 Bände. Übersetzung von Margarete Jacobi, Henny Koch und L. Ottmann. Leipzig: Hesse & Becker. 172, 285, 174, 333, 94, 94 S. mit Bildnis. Erschien auch in "Hesses Volksbücherei" als Nr. 649-660.

1912 Der berüchtigte (springende) Frosch der Grafschaft Calaveras und andere Erzählungen. Leipzig, Berlin: Heilbrunn & Co. 128 S. ("Albert Bonniers 30-Pfennig-Bücherei," Bd. XIV).

1913 Die Abenteuer des Tom Sawyer und Huckleberry Finn. Übersetzt von Ulrich Johannsen und Marie Schloss. Mit vielen Zeichnungen von E. Hirth. Strassburg i. E. und Leipzig: Singer. 615 S. ("Singer-Bücher," Bd. V).

1914 Tom Sawyers Abenteuer und Streiche. Übersetzung von Margarete Jacobi. Huckleberry Finns Abenteuer und Fahrten. Übersetzung von Henny Koch. Leipzig: Hesse & Becker. 285, 333 S. ("Romane der Weltliteratur").

Die Verschwörung von Fort Trumbull. Das Todeslos. Zürich: Verein für Verbreitung guter Schriften. 53 S. ("Verein für Verbreitung guter Schriften," Nr. 95).

1920 Tom Sawyers Abenteuer und Streiche. Übersetzt von Margarete Jacobi. Leipzig: Hesse & Becker. 285 S. ("Romane der Weltliteratur").
   Neudruck, 1925.
   Huckleberry Finns Abenteuer und Fahrten. Übersetzt von Henny Koch. Leipzig: Hesse & Becker. 333 S. ("Romane der Weltliteratur").
   Neudruck, 1925.
   Der gestohlene weisse Elefant. Humoreske. Leipzig: Reclam. 28 S. ("Reclams Automaten-Bücher," Nr. 34).
   Die Geschichte der kapitolinischen Venus und andere Skizzen. Leipzig: Reclam. 29 S. ("Reclams Automaten-Bücher," Nr. 33).

1921 Tom Sawyers Abenteuer. Hrsg. und übertragen von Ulrich Steindorff. Berlin: Ullstein. 333 S.
   Huckleberry Finns Fahrten und Abenteuer. Hrsg. und übertragen von Ulrich Steindorff. Berlin: Ullstein. 474 S.
   Der geheimnisvolle Fremde. Eine Phantasie. Übertragen von Wilhelm Nobbe. Leipzig: Insel-Verlag. 179 S.

1922 Bummel durch Europa. (A Tramp Abroad). Hrsg. und übertragen von Ulrich Steindorff. Berlin: Ullstein. 344 S.
   Durch Dick und Dünn. (Roughing It). Hrsg. und übertragen von Ulrich Steindorff. Berlin: Ullstein. 344 S.
   Die Abenteuer Tom Sawyers und Huckleberry Finns (des Kameraden von Tom Sawyer). Einleitung von Franz Kwest. Berlin: Mitteldeutsche Verlagsanstalt Lehmann & Fink. iv & 194, 236 S. ("Meistererzähler der Weltliteratur," Bd. XII).

1923 Tolle Geschichten. Hrsg. und übertragen von Ulrich Steindorff. Berlin: Ullstein. 279 S.
   Ein Yankee am Hofe des Königs Artus. Übersetzung von J. Botstiber und J. Ott. Umschlag und Federzeichnungen von Danilowatz. Wien: Stein-Verlag. 438 S. ("Die phantastischen Bücher," Bd. III).

1924 Mit heiteren Augen. Geschichten. Deutsche Übertragung von Margarete Jacobi, Henny Koch und L. Ottmann. Ausgewählt und eingeleitet von Ernst Preczang. Leipzig: Büchergilde Gutenberg. 192 S.
   Bummel durch das Mittelmeer. Deutsche Bearbeitung von Egon

Hannach. Leipzig: C. Stephenson. 320 S. ("Die lustigen Bücher," Bd. VI).

Kriegsgebet. In *Die Weltbühne*. Jg. 20, Nr. 47, Nov. 1924, S. 758.

Aus einem Wanderleben. 9 Skizzen. In *Die Kultur*. Jg. 2, H. 9, Juni 1924, S. 1-33.

1925 Tom Sawyers Abenteuer. Berlin: Schillerbuchhandlung. 271 S. ("Die bunten Romane der Weltliteratur," Bd. L).

Die Streiche Tom Sawyers und Huckleberry Finns. Übersetzung und Bearbeitung von Carl Hartz. Berlin: Deutsche Buchgemeinschaft. 361 S. ("Veröffentlichungen der Deutschen Buchgemeinschaft," Bd. LXXIX).

Nur für Mitglieder; nicht im Buchhandel.

Die Abenteuer Tom Sawyers. Mit einer Einleitung von Albert Erding. Berlin: M. Maschler. 300 S.

Die Abenteuer Huckleberry Finns (des Kameraden von Tom Sawyer). Mit einer Einleitung von Albert Erding. Berlin: M. Maschler. 347 S.

Mark Twain: Meine Uhr.—Max Maria von Weber: Eine Winternacht auf der Lokomotive. Berlin: H. Apitz. 32 S. in stenographischer Schrift. ("Kurzschriftliche Übungshefte," Heft 2).

1926 Humoristische Skizzen. Übersetzung von Margarete Krauss. Berlin: Weltgeist-Bücher. 63 S. ("Weltgeist-Bücher," Nr. 127).

Tom Sawyers Abenteuer und Streiche. Übersetzung von Margarete Jacobi. Leipzig: Hesse & Becker. 285 S. ("Die Schatzkammer," Bd. XLVI).

Neudruck 1930.

Huckleberry Finns Abenteuer und Fahrten. Übersetzung von Henny Koch. Leipzig: Hesse & Becker. 333 S. ("Die Schatzkammer," Bd. XLVII).

Neudruck 1930.

1927 Ausgewählte Skizzen. Deutsch von Wilhelm Lange. Bändchen I. Berlin: Buchhandlung des Stenographenverbandes Stolze-Schrey. 96 S. in stenographischer Schrift.

Humoresken. Übersetzung von Margarete Jacobi, Henny Koch und L. Ottmann. Textrevision von Lotte Blaschke. Leipzig: H. Fikentscher. 316 S. ("Hafis-Lesebücherei," Bd. XXVII).

Die Abenteuer des Tom Sawyer und Huckleberry Finn. Ins Deutsche übertragen, bearbeitet und mit einem Vorwort versehen von Walter Keiler. Leipzig: Zenith-Verlag. 291 S. ("Zenith-Bücherei").

1928 Tom Sawyers Abenteuer. Roman. Hamburg: Gesellschaft für Literatur, Leuchtfeuer-Verlag. 306 S.

Lustige Gefährten—tolle Sachen. Erzählungen und Skizzen. Übersetzung von Margarete Jacobi, Henny Koch und L. Ottmann.

Leipzig: Hesse & Becker. 172, 174 S. ("Die Schatzkammer," Bd. CXLVII).

Neudruck 1929 mit einer Lebensgeschichte Mark Twains und einem Nachwort von Ludwig Fürstenwerth. 172, 93, 93 S. ("Die Schatzkammer," Bd. CXLVIIa).

Ausgewählte Skizzen. Aus dem Englischen übertragen von Mira v. Hollander-Munkh. 88 S. Leipzig: Ph. Reclam jun. ("Reclams Universal-Bibliothek," Nr. 3749).

1929   Tom Sawyers Abenteuer. Übersetzung von R. Freund. Berlin: Die Buchgemeinde. ii & 271 S.

1933   Das Lächeln des Weisen. Die schönsten Humoresken. Einleitung, Auswahl und Übertragung von Günther Birkenfeld. Entwurf für Bucheinband und die Zeichnungen von Hans Koischwitz. Berlin: Deutsche Buchgemeinschaft. 409 S.

1935   Erzählungen. Hrsg. von Heinrich Gade. Bielefeld: Velhagen & Klasing. 48 S. ("Neusprachliche Lesebogen," Nr. 270).

1936   Die Abenteuer des Tom Sawyer. Neu bearbeitet nach der russischen Ausgabe des "Molodaja Gwardia" 1933 von D. Hollmann. Engels: Deutscher Staatsverlag. 225 S.

Die Abenteuer des Tom Sawyer und Huckleberry Finn. Übersetzung des ersten Teiles: Ulrich Johannsen; des zweiten Teiles: Marie Schloss. Illustrationen von Walter Trier. Berlin: Williams. 503 S.

APPENDIX II

ENGLISH EDITIONS OF MARK TWAIN'S WORKS APPEARING IN GERMANY
1876-1937

1876   The Adventures of Tom Sawyer. Leipsic: Tauchnitz. 303 pp. ("Collection of British Authors," Nr. 1622).

1879   The Innocents Abroad or The New Pilgrim's Progress. Two volumes. Leipsic: Tauchnitz. 320, 335 pp. ("Collection of British Authors," Nr. 1812-1813).

1880   Roughing It. Leipsic: Tauchnitz. 295 pp. ("Collection of British Authors," Nr. 1929).
       A Tramp Abroad. Two volumes. Leipsic: Tauchnitz. 288, 287 pp. ("Collection of British Authors," Nr. 1899-1900).

1881   The Innocents at Home. Leipsic: Tauchnitz. 286 pp. ("Collection of British Authors," Nr. 1948).
       The Prince and the Pauper. A Tale for Young People of all Ages. Two volumes. Leipsic: Tauchnitz. xiii & 232, 226 pp. ("Collection of British Authors," Nr. 2027-2028).
       Sketches. Zürich: Rudolphi & Klemm. 90 pp. ("English Library," Nr. I).

1882   The Stolen White Elefant etc. Leipsic: Tauchnitz. 288 pp. ("Collection of British Authors," Nr. 2077).

1883   Life on the Mississippi. Two volumes. Leipsic: Tauchnitz. 295, 270 pp. ("Collection of British Authors," Nr. 2143-2144).
       Sketches. With the portrait of the author. Leipsic: Tauchnitz. 351 pp. ("Collection of British Authors," Nr. 2162).

1885   The Adventures of Huckleberry Finn. (Tom Sawyer's Comrade). Two volumes. Leipsic: Tauchnitz. 270, 255 pp. ("Collection of British Authors," Nr. 2307-2308).

1886   Selections from American Humor. Leipsic: Tauchnitz. 287 pp. ("Collection of British Authors," Nr. 2529).

1890   A Yankee at the Court of King Arthur. Two volumes. Leipsic: Tauchnitz. 286, 270 pp. ("Collection of British Authors," Nr. 2638-2639).

1892   The American Claimant. Leipsic: Tauchnitz. 271 pp. ("Collection of British Authors," Nr. 2863).

1893   The Million-Pound Bank-Note and other New Stories. Leipsic: Tauchnitz. 280 pp. ("Collection of British Authors," Nr. 2907).

1894   Tom Sawyer Abroad. Illustrations by Dan Beard. Leipsic: Tauchnitz. 262 pp. ("Collection of British Authors," Nr. 2984).

1895   Pudd'nhead Wilson. Leipsic: Tauchnitz. 271 pp. ("Collection of British Authors," Nr. 3039).

1896   Personal Recollections of Joan of Arc by the Sieur Louis de Conte (her Page and Secretary), freely translated out of the ancient French into modern English from the original unpublished manuscript in the national archives of France by Jean Francois Alden. Two volumes. Leipsic: Tauchnitz. 279, 271 pp. ("Collection of British Authors," Nr. 3138-3139).

1897   More Tramps Abroad. Two volumes. Leipsic: Tauchnitz. 319, 319 pp. ("Collection of British Authors," Nr. 3252-3253).

Tom Sawyer, Detective, as told by Huck Finn, and other Tales. Leipsic: Tauchnitz. 255 pp. ("Collection of British Authors," Nr. 3184).

1900   The Man that Corrupted Hadleyburg, and other Stories and Sketches. Two volumes. Leipsic: Tauchnitz. 270, 287 pp. ("Collection of British Authors," Nr. 3453-3454).

1902   A Double-Barrelled Detective Story. Leipsic: Tauchnitz. 247 pp. ("Collection of British Authors," Nr. 3591).

1907   Christian Science. With Notes Containing Corrections to Date. Leipsic: Tauchnitz. 287 pp. ("Collection of British Authors," Nr. 3979).

The $30,000 Bequest and other Stories. Leipsic: Tauchnitz. 304 pp. ("Collection of British Authors," Nr. 3959).

1910   Extract from Captain Stormfield's Visit to Heaven. Is Shakespeare Dead? Leipsic: Tauchnitz. 256 pp. ("Collection of British Authors," Nr. 4209).

1916   Tom Sawyer, Detective, as told by Huck Finn. Copyright Edition. Leipsic: Tauchnitz. 127 pp. ("Tauchnitz Pocket Library," Nr. 75).

Sketches. Ser. 1. Leipsic: Tauchnitz. iii & 7-128 pp. ("English Textbooks," Nr. 32).

1918   Sketches. Ser. 2. Leipsic: Tauchnitz. iv & 129-351 pp. ("Tauchnitz Pocket Library," Nr. 88).

APPENDIX III

SCHOOL EDITIONS OF MARK TWAIN'S WORKS
APPEARING IN GERMANY
1895-1937

1895 The Prince and the Pauper. Edited and annotated by Dr. E. Lobedanz. Vocabulary. Berlin: Gärtner. vi & 165, 43 pp. ("Schulbibliothek französischer und englischer Prosaschriften aus der neueren Zeit," Nr. 15).

  2nd ed. (viii & 162 pp.), 1901; 3rd ed., 1909; 4th ed. (viii & 111 pp.), Berlin: Weidmannsche Buchhandlung, 1926.

1900 The Adventures of Tom Sawyer. Abridged edition. Edited by G. Krüger. Leipsic: Freytag. viii & 191 pp.

1901 The Prince and the Pauper. Selected and edited with notes, questions, and a vocabulary by Prof. Dr. Th. Lion. Dresden: Kühtmann. viii & 146, 38, 92 pp. ("English Library," Vol. XXXIV).

A Tramp Abroad. (Excerpts). Edited and annotated by Max Mann. Introduction by Max Mann. Leipsic: Freytag; Vienna: Tempsky. vi & 112, 46 pp.

1903 Kipling and Mark Twain. Five tales. Selected and edited with notes and a vocabulary by Fritz Kriete. Halle: Gesenius. vii & 83, 64 pp.

1906 A vocabulary for A Tramp Abroad. Arranged by Max Mann. Leipsic: Freytag. 46 pp.

1912 American Humor. W. Irving: Rip van Winkle; Bret Harte: Baby Sylvester; Mark Twain: How I Edited an Agricultural Paper. Leipsic: Jaeger. 72 pp. ("Sammlung englischer und französischer Autoren," Bd. XII).

1913 The Prince and the Pauper. Abridged edition. Edited by Rudolf Richter. Vienna: Tempsky; Leipsic: Freytag. 159 pp. ("Freytags Sammlung französischer und englischer Schriftsteller").

1914 The Prince and the Pauper. Edited with notes and an appendix by F. Roebbelen. Bielefeld & Leipsic: Velhagen & Klasing. x & 170, 34 pp. ("Velhagen & Klasings Sammlung französischer und englischer Schulausgaben. English Authors," Nr. 135B).

  2nd ed., 1919.

The Adventures of Tom Sawyer. Edited and annotated by H. Perschmann. With an appendix and a vocabulary. Bielefeld and Leipsic: Velhagen & Klasing. 124, 28, 52 pp. ("Velhagen & Klasings Sammlung französischer und englischer Schulausgaben. English Authors," Nr. 141B).

  Reprint 1925.

1925 The Adventures of Tom Sawyer. Edited with notes by H. Persch-
mann. With a portrait of the author. New edition with appendix.
Bielefeld and Leipsic: Velhagen & Klasing. x & 124, 28 pp.
("Velhagen & Klasings Sammlung französischer und englischer
Schulausgaben," Ausgabe B, Nr. 141).

1927 The Adventures of Tom Sawyer. Abridged edition by Hermann
Perschmann. Introduction and notes by Douglas Yates. With one
portrait. Bielefeld and Leipsic: Velhagen & Klasing. vii & 124,
27 pp. ("Velhagen & Klasings Sammlung französischer und eng-
lischer Schulausgaben. Reform-Ausgaben," Bd. LVII).
Cecil Rhodes. Annotated by Karl Holtermann. Münster i. W.:
Aschendorffsche Verlaghandlung. Nr. 5 of "Six Modern Standard
Novels." ("Aschendorffs moderne Auslandsbücherei").

1930 The Death-Disk. Edited by Dr. Friedrich Meyer. Frankfurt a.
M.: Diesterweg. 15 pp. ("Diesterwegs neusprachliche Lesehefte,"
Nr. 181).
5th ed., 1935.

BIBLIOGRAPHY

Only those publications are cited which have been of direct aid in the investigation.

Bauch, Reinhold. Englisches Lesebuch zur Einführung in Kultur- und Geistesleben. Tl. 2. Die Literatur der Vereinigten Staaten von Amerika. Dresden, 1926.

Baumann, Fritz. "Mark Twain." *National-Zeitung,* Nov. 30, 1905.

Beilage zur Allgemeinen Zeitung, (Munich), May 6, 1896.

Berges, Philipp. "Mark Twain." *Norddeutsche Allgemeine Zeitung. Unterhaltungsbeilage,* Nov. 30, 1905.

Bierbaum, F. P. History of the English Language and Literature from the Earliest Times until the Present Day including the American Literature. 2nd ed. Heidelberg, 1889.

Birkenfeld, Günther. Introduction to Das Lächeln des Weisen. Die schönsten Humoresken. Berlin, 1933.

Bleibtreu, Karl. Geschichte der englischen Literatur mit Einschluss der amerikanischen. Bern, 1923.

Brandl, Alois. Review of Schönemann's Mark Twain als literarische Persönlichkeit. *Die Literatur,* XXVII (1924-1925), 627 f.

Bratter, C. A. "Mark Twain, der Klassiker des amerikanischen Humors." *B.Z. am Mittag,* April 22, 1910.

Bratter, C. A. "Amerikas Meister-Humorist." *Vossische Zeitung,* June 25, 1921.

Brattskoven, Otto. "Mark Twains Erscheinung. Zu seinem 20. Todestag am 21. April." *Fränkische Tagespost,* April 22, 1930.

Bütow, Hans. "Mark Twain:—zur 100. Wiederkehr seines Geburtstages am 30. November." *Frankfurter Zeitung,* Nov. 30, 1935.

Conrad, Michael Georg. "Der Humorist Mark Twain." *Die Gesellschaft,* Nov. 1893, pp. 1504-1508.

Dick, E. "Aus Mark Twains Leben." *Zeitschrift für französischen und englischen Unterricht,* XVI (1917), 171-183.

Diederich, Benno. "Mark Twain und der amerikanische Humor." *Der Türmer,* July 1903, pp. 434-445.

Diederich, Benno. "Mark Twain." *Tägliche Rundschau,* Nov. 30, 1905, pp. 1117 ff.

Diederich, Benno. "Neues vom alten Mark Twain." *Der Türmer,* May 1906, pp. 173-178.

Doehn, Rudolf. Aus dem amerikanischen Dichterwald. Leipsic, 1881.

Eick, Hugo. "Mark Twain." *März,* IV, 2 (May 1910), 314-317.

Ellinger, J. Review of the school edition of *The Prince and the Pauper* by E. Lobedanz. *Anglia: Beiblatt,* VI (1895-1896), 45 ff.

Ellinger, J. Review of Schönemann's Mark Twain als literarische Persönlichkeit. *Anglia: Beiblatt*, XXXVI (1925), 372 ff.

Elster, Hanns Martin. "Ein Mann lehrt Amerika lachen." *Rheinisch Westfälische Zeitung*, Nov. 27, 1935.

Engel, Eduard. "Mark Twain. Ein amerikanischer Humorist." *Magazin für die Literatur des Auslandes*, Oct. 9, 1880, pp. 575-579.

Engel, Eduard. "Mark Twain: *Roughing It*." *Magazin für die Literatur des Auslandes*, Nov. 27, 1880, p. 681.

Engel, Eduard. "Mark Twain: *Der Prinz und der Bettler*." *Magazin für die Literatur des In- und Auslandes*, May 6, 1882, pp. 259-261.

Engel, Eduard. Geschichte der englischen Literatur. Appendix: Geschichte der Literatur Nordamerikas. 8th ed. Leipsic, 1915.

Engel, Eduard. Geschichte der Literatur Nordamerikas. Leipsic, no date.

Engel, H. "Eine persönliche Erinnerung an Mark Twain." *Zeitschrift für französischen und englischen Unterricht*, XVI (1917), 357 f.

Evans, E. P. Beiträge zur amerikanischen Literatur- und Kulturgeschichte. Stuttgart, 1898.

Feldkeller, Paul. "Mark Twain." *Leipziger Neueste Nachrichten*, Nov. 30, 1935.

Fischer, Rudolf. Review of *Personal Recollections of Joan of Arc* (Tauchnitz ed.). *Archiv für das Studium der neueren Sprachen*, XCIX (1897), 131 ff.

Fischer, Rudolf. Review of *Is Shakespeare Dead?*. *Jahrbuch der deutschen Shakespeare-Gesellschaft*, XLVI (1910), 258 f.

Fischer, Walther. Review of Schönemann's Mark Twain als literarische Persönlichkeit. *Englische Studien*, LXI (1926), 135-139.

Fischer, Walther. Amerikanische Prosa. Vom Bürgerkrieg bis auf die Gegenwart (1863-1922). Leipsic, 1926.

Fischer, Walther. Die englische Literatur der Vereinigten Staaten von Nordamerika. Potsdam, 1929.

Fischer, Walther. "Mark Twain. Zu seinem 100.Geburtstage am 30.Nov. 1935." *Die Neueren Sprachen*, XLIII (1935), 471-480.

Flügel, Ewald. Die nordamerikanische Literatur. Leipsic, Wien, 1907.

Förster, Brix. "Aus Mark Twains Autobiographie." *Allgemeine Zeitung*, May 21, 1910, pp. 405 ff.

Frapan, Ilse. "Neues von dem amerikanischen Humoristen." *Magazin für die Literatur des In- und Auslandes*, June 30, 1883, pp. 374-377.

Friedmann, Dr. "Amerikanische Humoristen." *Magazin für die Literatur des Auslandes*, LXXXIX (April 22, 1876), 239-242.

Friedmann, Dr. "Neue Folge der amerikanischen Humoristen." *Magazin für die Literatur des Auslandes*, XCII (Sept. 8, 1877), 548 ff.

Friedmann, Dr. "Ein Humorist auf Reisen." *Magazin für die Literatur des Auslandes*, LXXXIX (April 29, 1876), 262.

Fürst, Rudolf. "Mark Twain zum 70. Geburtstag." *Vossische Zeitung,* Nov. 1905.

von Gottberg, O. "Mark Twain." *Velhagen & Klasings Monatshefte,* June 1910, pp. 270-274.

von Gottberg, O. "Mark Twain." *Berliner Lokal-Anzeiger,* April 22, 1910.

Harbeck, Hans. "Amerikanischer Humor." *Der Kreis* (Hamburg), IV (1927), 276 ff.

Heim, Hans. Review of the school edition of *The Adventures of Tom Sawyer* by G. Krüger (1900). *Anglia: Beiblatt,* XII (Jan. 1901), 28-31.

Henderson, Archibald. "Mark Twain—wie er ist." *Deutsche Revue,* XXXIV (Nov. 1909), 195-205.

Henderson, Archibald. "Mark Twain als Philosoph, Moralist und Soziologe." *Deutsche Revue,* XXXVI (Feb. 1911), 189-205.

Holzer, Gustav. "Mark Twain und Shakespeare." *Heidelberger Tageblatt,* June 26, 1909, pp. 3-8.

Huendgen. Review of the school edition of *A Tramp Abroad* by Max Mann. *Gymnasium,* XXIII (1905), 49 f.

Hüppy, August. "Mark Twains Reisebuch: *A Tramp Abroad* oder *Reise in der Fremde."* *Alte und neue Welt,* LIX (1924-1925), 338-342.

Hüppy, August. Mark Twain und die Schweiz, dem grossen Freund und Bewunderer unseres Landes zum 100. Geburtstag gewidmet. Zürich, 1935.

von Jan, Eduard. "Das literarische Bild der Jeanne D'Arc." *Beihefte zur Zeitschrift für romanische Philologie,* LXXVI (1928), 139-144; 187.

Jensen, Joh. V. "Mark Twain." *Frankfurter Zeitung,* April 26, 1910.

Keller, Helen. "Mark Twain, wie ich ihn kannte." *Münchner Post. Unterhaltungsblatt,* Jan. 15, 1930.

Kellner, Leon. "Mark Twain." *Neue Freie Presse,* Dec. 3, 1905, pp. 31 f.

Kellner, Leon. Geschichte der nordamerikanischen Literatur. Vol. II. Berlin, 1913.

Kindt, Hermann. "Moderne amerikanische Humoristen." *Die Gegenwart,* XXX (July 24, 1886), 53 ff.

Klein, Tim. "Bildnis von Mark Twain." *Münchener Neueste Nachrichten,* Nov. 30, 1935.

Knortz, Karl. Geschichte der nordamerikanischen Literatur. 2 vols. Berlin, 1891.

Körting, Gustav. Grundriss der Geschichte der englischen Literatur. Münster i.W., 1887: 2nd ed. 1893: 4th ed. 1905.

Krebs, Kurt G. "Amerikanischer Humor." *Hellweg,* Aug. 10, 1927.

Krummacher, M. Review of the school edition of *The Adventures of*

Tom Sawyer by G. Krüger (1900). *Die Neueren Sprachen,* IX (Jan. 1902), 546 f.

Landau, Paul. "Mark Twain und der amerikanische Humor." *Beilage zur Allgemeinen Zeitung,* Nov. 30, 1905.

Landau, Paul. "Mark Twain." *Norddeutsche Allgemeine Zeitung,* April 24, 1910.

Lange, Wilhelm. Preface to Vol. I of *Ausgewählte Skizzen* von Mark Twain. Leipsic, 1878.

Lenz, Werner. "Ein treuer Freund Deutschlands." *Berliner Börsen-Zeitung,* Nov. 29, 1935.

Lipton, Eduard. "Mark Twain." *Wiener Deutsches Tagblatt,* Nov. 30, 1905.

Lobedanz, E. Introduction and preface to his edition of *The Prince and the Pauper.* Berlin, 1895.

von Lossow, Rudolf. "Mark Twain und Wir." *Berliner Börsen-Zeitung,* Nov. 29, 1935.

Lüdeke, Henry. Reviews of The Ordeal of Mark Twain by Van Wyck Brooks and Mark Twain als literarische Persönlichkeit by F. Schönemann. *Deutsche Literaturzeitung,* N.F. II (Sept. 12, 1925), 1802-1813.

Ludwig, Albert. Review of *Huckleberry Finns Fahrten und Abenteuer* (Ullstein ed.). *Das literarische Echo,* XXIV (May 1, 1922), 943 f.

Manuel, Bruno. "Im Schatten des Titanen." Vorspiele zu Mark Twains 100.Geburtstag. *Leipziger Neueste Nachrichten,* Sept. 17, 1935.

Michaud, Regis. Die amerikanische Literatur der Gegenwart. Leipsic, 1931.

Monatsblätter für deutsche Literatur, III (1898-1899), 33 ff.

Müller, Ad. Review of the school edition of *The Prince and the Pauper* by E. Lobedanz. *Archiv für das Studium der neueren Sprachen und Literaturen,* XCV (1895), 312 f.

Müller, Carl. "Mark Twain." *Hamburgischer Correspondent,* Nov. 30, 1905.

Osterburg-Verakoff, Max. "Mark Twain." *Die Gesellschaft,* Oct. 1890, pp. 1549 f.

Paine, Albert Bigelow. Mark Twain, a Biography. 3 vols. New York, 1912.

Pötzl, Eduard. "Mark Twain." *Neues Wiener Tagblatt,* Nov. 30, 1905.

Preczang, Ernst. Introduction to the Büchergilde Gutenberg edition of *Mit heiteren Augen. Geschichten.* Leipsic, 1924.

Rambeau, A. Preface to M. Fischer's article "Mark Twain on Christian Science." *Die Neueren Sprachen,* XVII (1909-1910), 206-228.

Saager, A. "Mark Twain." *Hamburger Nachrichten,* Nov. 29, 1905.

Sack, E. L. "Mark Twain." *Der Bund. Berner Zeitung,* Nov. 1935.

Salomon, Ludwig. "Mark Twain." *Illustrierte Zeitung*, Oct. 6, 1888, pp. 345 f.

Salomon, Ludwig. "Mark Twain, zu seinem 70. Geburtstag." *Illustrierte Zeitung*, Nov. 30, 1905, pp. 836 f.

Salten, Felix. "Mark Twain." *Pester Lloyd*, April 23, 1910.

Sastre, Enrique. "Mark Twain." *Volksbühnen-Blätter*, III (1926), 102 f.

Scherr, Johannes. Illustrierte Geschichte der Weltliteratur. 6th ed. 1880.

Schidlof, B. "Zum Tode Mark Twains." *Aus fremden Zungen*, XX (1910), 524 ff.

Schleich, Karl Ludwig. "Psychophysik des Humors." *Die Zukunft*, Nov. 19, 1898, pp. 374-393.

Schönbach, Anton E. Über die humoristische Prosa des XIX. Jahrhunderts. Graz., 1875.

Schönbach, Anton E. "Über die amerikanische Romandichtung der Gegenwart." *Deutsche Rundschau*, XLVI (March, 1886), 416-433.

Schönbach, Anton E. Gesammelte Aufsätze zur neueren Literatur in Deutschland, Österreich, Amerika. Graz, 1900.

Schönemann, Friedrich. Review of *Tolle Geschichten* (Ullstein ed.). *Die Literatur*, XXVI (Oct. 1923-Sept. 1924), 179.

Schönemann, Friedrich. Review of *Bummel durch Europa* (Ullstein ed.). *Das literarische Echo*, XXV (Oct. 1922-Sept. 1923), 177.

Schönemann, Friedrich. Review of *Durch Dick und Dünn* (Ullstein ed.). *Das literarische Echo*, XXV (Oct. 1922-Sept. 1923), 1127.

Schönemann, Friedrich. "Amerikanischer Humor." *Germanisch-Romanische Monatsschrift*, VIII (1920), 152-164; 216-227.

Schönemann, Friedrich. "Mark Twains Weltanschauung." *Englische Studien*, LV (1921), 53-84.

Schönemann, Friedrich. "Mr. Samuel Langhorne Clemens." *Archiv für das Studium der neueren Sprachen und Literaturen*, CXLIV (1922-1923), 184-213.

Schönemann, Friedrich. "Mark Twains Autobiographie." *Hannoverscher Kurier*, Aug. 5, 1925; also *Magdeburger Zeitung*, Oct. 4, 1925.

Schönemann, Friedrich. Mark Twain als literarische Persönlichkeit. (*Jenaer Germanistische Forschungen*, VIII). Jena, 1925.

Schönemann, Friedrich. "Mark Twain und Deutschland." *Hochschule und Ausland*, XIV (1936), 37-43.

Schönemann, Friedrich. "Mark Twain—ein Freund Deutschlands." *Deutsche Allgemeine Zeitung*, Nov. 24, 1935.

Schönemann, Friedrich. "Neue Mark Twain-Studien." *Die Neueren Sprachen*, XLIV (1936), 260-272.

Seidel, H. Wolfgang. "Erinnerung an Mark Twain." *Der Tag*, July 25, 1924.

Sil-Vara. "Die Autobiographie Mark Twains." *Neue Freie Presse,* Aug. 13, 1925.

Sinclair, Upton. "Der ungekrönte König." Translation by Hermynia zur Mühlen. *Frankfurter Zeitung,* Aug. 12, 1925.

Sintenis, Franz. Literarische Ansichten in Vorträgen. Jurjew, 1894.

Smith, Charles Alphonso. Die amerikanische Literatur, Vorlesungen gehalten an der Königlichen Friedrich-Wilhelms-Universität zu Berlin. (Vol. II of the "Bibliothek der amerikanischen Kulturgeschichte"). Berlin, 1912.

Steindorff, Ulrich. "Mark Twain's Broad German Grin." *The New York Times Book Review,* July 13, 1924.

Steindorff, Ulrich. Introduction to his edition of *Tom Sawyers Abenteuer.* Berlin, 1921.

Stern, Adolf. "Sternbannerserie." *Magazin für die Literatur des In- und Auslandes,* March 30, 1889, pp. 211-214.

Swoboda, Wilhelm. Review of the school edition of *A Tramp Abroad* by Max Mann (1903). *Die Neueren Sprachen,* XI (1903-1904), 223 ff.

von Thaler, Carl. "Mark Twain in Deutschland." *Die Gegenwart,* LX (1899), 376 ff.

Thiess, Frank. "Einem fröhlichen Mann zum 100.Geburtstag." *Königsberger Allgemeine Zeitung,* Nov. 30, 1935.

Wagner, Ph. Review of the school edition of *The Adventures of Tom Sawyer* by K. Krüger (1900). *Englische Studien,* XXX (1902), 164 f.

Walter, G. A. "Mark Twain zum Gedenken." *Kölner Volkszeitung,* Nov. 30, 1935.

Willinsky, G. "Mark Twain." Zum 100.Geburtstag des grossen amerikanischen Humoristen am 30.November. *Magdeburger Zeitung,* Nov. 30, 1935.

Wülker, Richard. Review of *A Yankee at the Court of King Arthur.* *Anglia: Beiblatt,* II (April 1, 1891), 10 f.

Wurm, A. "Mark Twain als Mensch und Humorist." *Alte und neue Welt,* XXXVIII (1903-1904), 718-720; 748-751.

Zupitza, Julius. Review of *A Yankee at the Court of King Arthur* (Tauchnitz ed.). *Archiv für das Studium der neueren Sprachen und Literaturen,* LXXXV (1890), 99-102.

INDEX